Richard P. Vaughan

Basic Skills
for Christian Counselors

An Introduction for
Pastoral Ministers

paulist press *new york / mahwah*

Library of Congress Cataloging-in-Publication Data

Vaughan, Richard P. (Richard Patrick), 1919–
    Basic skills for Christian counselors.

    Bibliography: p.
    1. Pastoral counseling.   2. Pastoral theology—Catholic Church.
3. Catholic Church—Clergy.   I. Title.
BV4012.2.V378   1986   253.5   86-25491
ISBN 0-8091-2857-8

Published by Paulist Press
997 Macarthur Boulevard
Mahwah, New Jersey 07430

Printed and bound in the United States of America

Contents

Preface

In 1969 I wrote *An Introduction to Religious Counseling* which dealt extensively with the psychological foundations of pastoral counseling but ignored, for the most part, process, skills, and strategies in counseling. Shortly after writing this book I began a new career, first in university and then in church administration. Ten years later, I took a sabbatical and attended classes at UCLA so as to prepare myself to reenter the fields of counseling and teaching. While at UCLA I discovered a new approach to counseling and teaching others how to counsel. This approach concentrated on counseling skills and strategies as building blocks in the counseling process. After using this approach in my counseling practice and teaching it to my students in counseling psychology, it struck me that it could be a most useful tool for those engaged in pastoral counseling or aspiring to become pastoral counselors.

In the beginning, I intended simply to rewrite *An Introduction to Religious Counseling* and then add a section dealing with counseling skills and strategies. As the project progressed, it became clear that the direction I was taking was very different from the original book and that much of the original book would add little to the new work, and so I abandoned my plan to revise *An Introduction to Religous Counseling* and concentrated my efforts to produce a new work. Parts of the original book, however, seemed to serve well as background material for an explanation of counseling skills and strategies, such as the chapter on Feelings and Emotions, a section in the chapter on Coping and another on the Nature of Religious Counseling, which have been rewritten and constitute a part of the present work.

Were it not for my students and counselees, this work would never have come to fruition. The positive reaction and subsequent success of my graduate students who have learned and applied the counseling skills and strategies have proven to me that this new way of teaching counseling can be most effective; the response of counselees to my efforts to help them has also proven to me that skills and strategies play an important part in the process of counseling. Therefore, I am much indebted to the students whom I have taught for the past nine years and the people I have counseled during this same period.

I have made every effort to avoid sexist language. If I have failed, it is not intentional. Some key skills and strategies have been explained a second time but in a different context. *Repetitio est mater studiorum.* (Repetition is the mother of learning.) This book is meant to be a learning tool for both those aspiring to become counselors in pastoral ministry and those already engaged in this ministry. It is my hope that repetition will strengthen the learning process.

I wish to express my gratitude to the Rev. Robert Caro, S. J. for his encouragement, the Rev. Rockwell Shaules, S. J. and Rev. Leo Rock, S. J. for their comments on the manuscript, and Brother Henry Yoshioka, S. J. for his technical assistance in producing this book.

1

Introduction and Overview

Counseling is a dialogue between a helping person and someone who seeks help. It is one of many services offered by men and women engaged in pastoral ministry; other forms of pastoral ministry are celebrating the liturgy, taking the Eucharist to shut-ins, teaching religion to adults and children, consoling the bereaved, and visiting the sick. Counseling is, therefore, one of many ministries undertaken by dedicated men and women in the Church. It is an important ministry because it assists people in finding solutions to their daily problems on the basis of their Christian commitment and thus to live fuller Christian lives.

In the past, pastoral ministry usually referred to the work of priests and ministers. In the last couple of decades, however, sisters and lay men and women have entered the field of pastoral ministry. Today some sisters hold the position of associate pastor in parishes; others are pastoral ministers in hospitals and on university campuses. A few of them are directors of campus and hospital ministry or fill administrative positions in the Church. To a lesser extent, lay men and women hold some of these same positions in the Catholic community. As the number of clergy decreases due to a sharp decline in the number of priests ordained each year, it is quite likely that sisters and lay people will play an ever increasing role in pastoral ministry. Among Protestant groups, women have become ministers, and both lay men and women have assumed a more active role in the pastoral ministry, with pastoral counseling being a part of this ministry. This book addresses not only priests and ministers but also the sisters and lay people who are presently in pastoral counseling or hope to become pastoral counselors. Even though the book is written by a Catholic who is engaged in both pastoral and psychological counseling, it is my hope that it will be of value to members of all Christian groups who are or wish to be pastoral counselors.

PRIESTS AND MINISTERS AS COUNSELORS

In many seminaries formal training in pastoral counseling is limited or even absent. Few seminaries either Catholic or Protestant offer a program of courses on the principles and techniques of counseling joined with supervised practice, such as one finds in the training of clinical and counseling psychologists. Within the Catholic Church, it is generally accepted that the philosophical and theological education plus a couple of courses in psychology which the clergy received in the seminary adequately equips them to counsel the people they meet in parishes, hospitals or on the university campuses. However, once newly ordained priests have worked in the ministry for a while, many of them discover how inadequately prepared they are to help people in times of distress and crisis. Even though they have a strong desire to help those who come to them for assistance, they find that they are often wanting in the counseling skills needed for this ministry. An exception are the clergy, religious and lay men and women who have taken the Clinical Pastoral Experience (CPE) which is offered to those who are preparing themselves for hospital ministry. In the CPE, priests, nuns and some lay people learn the basic skills needed for pastoral ministry in a hospital setting and are supervised as they apply these skills. In the Protestant seminaries, there appears to be a greater stress on training in pastoral counseling than in the Catholic seminaries; as a consequence, the Protestant clergy seem to be better prepared for this ministry.

PREPARATION OF SISTERS AND LAY PEOPLE

Aside from the CPE, most sisters and lay people entering the field of pastoral counseling also seem to have limited training in counseling. Since both the nuns and the lay men and women usually have college degrees and have completed several courses in theology and psychology, they are generally considered adequately prepared for pastoral counseling. It is presumed that experience and a couple of workshops in pastoral psychology or counseling will make up for any deficiencies in training they may have. In the Protestant churches, however, there is gradual growth in programs in pastoral counseling and supervised experience for the lay people who have been selected on the basis of their Christian commitment and intend to enter the field of pastoral counseling.

This book cannot take the place of a systematic program in counseling and make up for deficiencies in counselor training, but it may serve as a textbook for a course in pastoral counseling and also help counselors who have never had formal training in counseling become acquainted with the basic procedures in pastoral counseling. Hopefully, this book will also offer these latter people the opportunity to learn about some of the basic counseling skills and techniques that are the foundation of all effective counseling, encourage them to incorporate these skills and techniques into their practice, discover and correct faulty counseling procedures they may have developed, and finally improve their over-all effectiveness as pastoral counselors.

AN ART OR A SCIENCE?

Whether counseling is an art or a science is a controversial issue. In all likelihood it is a combination of both. As an art, counseling is a natural talent which allows some people to be more effective in helping others; as a science, it is the product of scientific research dealing with what takes place in a counseling session. With the advent of audio and video recordings, research in counseling took a gigantic step forward. Literally thousands of counseling sessions have been recorded and analyzed by expert counselors who have attempted to cull out the basic skills and techniques used by effective counselors. These researchers have carefully defined each of these skills and techniques and developed methods of teaching them to trainees.[1] These skills and procedures will be presented in this book and then it will be shown how they apply to the field of pastoral counseling.

Counseling as an art cannot be taught; it is an ability one has or does not have. Twenty-five years ago, counseling was considered primarily an art. After a few basic courses in psychology, those wishing to try their hand at counseling were assigned four or five clients and a supervisor. If they had a natural talent for counseling, they generally did well; if they did not, they usually dropped out and tried some other profession. This philosophy of counseling education may have influenced the view of seminary administrators and convinced them that priests and ministers need little or no formal training in counseling to handle the type of person they usually see in a parish or hospital. If the priest or minister had a natural talent for counseling, he would probably do well regardless of the type of training he had received and the people of the parish or hospital would look to him for counseling; if he did not have a natural talent for counseling, training would make little difference and the priest would probably avoid pastoral counseling as much as possible and spend his energies in other ministries.

QUALITIES OF THE SUCCESSFUL COUNSELOR

After analyzing hundreds of recordings of psychologists and psychiatrists, Carkhuff and his associates have determined the specific characteristics of successful counselors and psychotherapists.[2] They found that successful counselors are empathetic, genuine, and manifest respect for the people they are trying to help. They then developed scales to measure the level of functioning on each of these qualities. While some people were naturally more empathetic, genuine, and respectful than others, these researchers maintained that all can learn these characteristics and that lay people, such as college graduates or volunteer workers in hospitals, can sometimes learn them more rapidly and fully than some psychiatrists and psychologists.[3]

EMPATHETIC

People are empathetic when they are able "to be with" the other person and to understand that person's inner world. They try to see the other's inner world as that person sees it. The Indians had a phrase which described empathy as "walking in another person's moccasins."[4] In other words, it is as if the empathetic person crawls inside the other person's skin and tries to understand just how that person feels and sees the world of people or things about him or her. The empathetic person not only sees things the way the other person sees them but also communicates verbally to the other person that he or she understands how this other person sees them.

In describing a good empathetic response, Carkhuff states: "The helper responds with accurate understanding of the surface feelings of the helpee but may not respond to or may misinterpret the deeper feelings. The expressions of the helper in response to the expressions of the helpee are essentially interchangeable with those of the helpee in that they express essentially the same meaning."[5] In this case, the counselor is aware of the counselee's expressed feelings and lets the counselee know, usually through verbal communication, that he or she understands how the counselee feels. Carkhuff describes a superior empathetic response as one in which "the helper communicates his understanding of the expressions of the helpee at a level deeper than they expressed and thus enables the helpee to experience and express feelings he was unable to express previously."[6] The response of the helper adds noticeably to the expression of the helpee in such a way as to express feelings at a level deeper than the helpee was able to express himself. For the most part, pastoral counseling deals with reflecting surface feelings, whereas psychotherapy tries to help people express feelings and emotions that were previously unrecognized. Being empathetic is an essential characteristic of the effective pastoral counselor and psychotherapist; they simply work at different levels of empathy.

GENUINE

People who are genuine demonstrate sincerity, openness and spontaneity. "Genuine people are at home with themselves and therefore can comfortably be themselves in all their interactions. This means that they do not have to change when they are with different people—that is, they do not have to constantly adopt new roles in order to be acceptable to others."[7] They are without front or facade. People who are genuine are aware of their own feelings and attitudes and unafraid to manifest these feelings and attitudes at the appropriate time.

Carkhuff describes a high level of genuineness in the following way: "The helper responds with many of his own feelings and there is no doubt as to whether he really means what he says," and "The helper is clearly being himself and employing his own genuine responses constructively."[8] In describing a lack of genuineness, Carkhuff states: "There is evidence of a considerable discrepancy between the helper's inner experiencing and his current verbalizations."[9] In other words, what the person says and what he or she actually thinks and feels are two different things.

RESPECT

People show respect for others when they demonstrate by their behavior and actions that they value or prize these other individuals. Respect follows from an appreciation of the human dignity and worth of the individual with whom we are dealing. It means that we care about and see something in this person that makes us respect him or her as a valuable person.

Carkhuff describes a high level of respect as follows: "The helper communicates a very deep caring for the feelings, experiences, and potentials of the helpee," and "The helper cares very deeply for the human potentials of the helpee and communicates a commitment to enabling the helpee to actualize this potential."[10]

Respect is an attitude that one person has for another. Egan says: "Respect is not often communicated directly in words in helping situations. Actions speak louder than words. For instance, the helper seldom if ever says, 'I respect you because you are a human being,' 'I prize you,' or 'I respect you for engaging in self-exploration. You are doing a good thing.' Respect is communicated principally by the ways helpers orient themselves toward and work with clients."[11] People show respect for others by indicating, often indirectly, that they are for this other person and want to give their time and effort to help this other person. What they are doing is not simply something they must do because it is their job or the circumstances in which they find themselves demand it. They are doing for the other person because they respect that person's dignity and worth as a fellow human being; they care and want to help that person as a prized individual.

WARMTH

In addition to being empathetic, genuine and having respect for the person you are counseling, some researchers have discovered a fourth quality of the successful counselors, namely, they show warmth toward the counselee. "Warmth is the physical expression of empathy (understanding) and respect (caring). It is generally communicated through a wide variety of non-verbal media such as gestures, posture, tone of voice, touch, or facial expression."[12] Warmth is a difficult quality to define but it is something we have all experienced. It is friendliness but at the same time more than just being friendly. The warm person is one who gives you the impression that he or she is happy to see you, interested in you for what you are, and cares about you. Warmth is a feeling that we have toward another; it is difficult, if not impossible, to fake this feeling by imitating the tone of voice or gestures of a warm person. One can learn how to be empathetic and to show respect for another, which are parts of warmth, and with considerable effort imitate the non-verbal dimensions of warmth but none of these is likely to make the counselor feel warm toward the counselee, and somehow the counselee picks up that the warmth is not genuine.

ATTENDING, LISTENING AND REFLECTING SKILLS

Research shows that successful counselors usually have developed a number of basic communication skills that are the foundation for other counseling procedures and techniques. Some of these skills are attending, listening and reflecting, which include such procedures as (1) Reading Non-Verbal and Paraverbal Communication, such as body language, gestures and tone of voice, (2) Understanding and Reflecting Content, Feelings and Meaning in the counselee's message, (3) Using Questions, (4) Using Encouragement Statements, (5) Perception Checking and (6) Summarizing. Each of these skills can be learned, and they are the building blocks upon which rests the total counseling process. Allen Ivey has devised a program which teaches prospective counselors these skills.[13] Once the basic counseling skills are learned, mostly through practical exercises, then the student learns to put them all together and use them in a counseling session.

INFLUENCING SKILLS

Attending and listening skills set the stage for influencing skills. Influencing skills attempt to have counselees change how they think, act and relate to others or their environment. They aim at getting counselees to look at their typical ways of thinking, acting and relating and then decide whether they need to change these ways so as to solve a problem they face. The influencing skills which pertain to pastoral counseling are: (1) Giving Information, (2) Instructing, (3) Reassuring, (4) Confronting, (5) Leading, and (6) Suggesting and Giving Advice.

A PROBLEM SOLVING TECHNIQUE

People who come for pastoral counseling often have a problem and are seeking a solution for the problem. Psychologists have developed a technique for assisting people in solving their problems.[14] The technique makes use of a structured schema of topics beginning with a description and definition of the person's problem and how he or she feels about it. The schema then treats the goal of the process and reasons why the person wants to solve the problem since some people really do not want to solve their problem, even though they say they do. Then the person is asked to consider possible ways the problem could be solved, which become options. Each of these options is evaluated on the basis of what seems to favor it and what seems against adopting it. At the urging of the counselor the individual is encouraged to consider how his or her values are related to each of these options. Once each possible option has been thoroughly discussed, the counselee is asked to decide upon the one which looks best and is most likely to solve the problem. This process is followed by a discussion of ways to implement the decision the counselee has made. In the problem solving technique the counselor acts as a facilitator who assists the counselee in deciding upon the way to solve his or her problem but the counselor does not give advice as to how the problem should be solved.

SUPPORTIVE MEASURES

Some people who seek counseling either have no problem or realize that there is no immediate solution to the problem they presently face; yet they are convinced that counseling can help them. At times all of us find ourselves under great stress and in need of support from another person. We look for someone to tell us that we have the strength to weather the storm and continue to live productive lives. Psychiatrists and psychologists sometimes use a technique called supportive therapy, which pastoral counselors can also use when people come to them not to help them solve their problems but just for emotional support in a time of distress.

MAKING A REFERRAL

At times pastoral counselors are asked to help people whose mental and emotional condition call for assistance beyond their expertise and thus need to be referred to a psychiatrist, psychologist or marriage counselor. It is, therefore, important that pastoral counselors know whom they can and whom they cannot help, which means that they should have an understanding of the different types of mental and emotional disorders they are apt to meet in their counseling practice and the type of professional to whom they should refer these disturbed counselees. Since the way a referral is made may determine the success or failure of future psychotherapy, how it is made is very important.

HOW TO USE THIS BOOK

In addition to describing the nature and components of pastoral counseling, this book introduces you to basic communication skills and some techniques commonly used by psychologists and psychiatrists. Reading about these skills and techniques and how and when to use them can help you become a better counselor. However, educators in counseling have found that the best way to become a more effective counselor is to practice these skills and techniques with two or three others who are also interested in becoming counselors. In these exercises, each member of the group takes a turn at counseling and being counseled, and each receives feedback from the other members of the group after he or she has been the counselor. The sessions can be tape recorded and reviewed either later by the one doing the counseling or immediately by the group, depending upon the amount of time available to the group. The subject matter for the counseling sessions is usually some kind of difficulty or problem we all are apt to encounter in our everyday life, such as a problem we have at work or in relating to a friend, or it can be a made-up difficulty with which the person playing the part of the counselee can identify. In each exercise the group concentrates on one or more communication skills; once the basic communication skills have been mastered, the group works on counseling techniques.

While students in pastoral counseling will find the approach described above most helpful, this approach is most probably not practical for the person presently engaged in pastoral ministry because of the amount of time it requires. Counselors in pastoral ministry whose time for professional development is limited will find profitable reading about the skills and techniques and making a concerted effort to incorporate these skills and techniques into their style of counseling. If they have the opportunity to tape some of their counseling sessions and later review them so as to evaluate their use of the skills and techniques, they will probably derive even greater benefit. One way to learn from a taped counseling session is to jot down what you should have said each time you hear a response you do not like. Over the course of years, most counselors develop their own style which may be already effective but could become even more effective by incorporating some of the skills and techniques described and exemplified in this book.

COMMON PROBLEMS
PASTORAL COUNSELORS MEET

In this book the skills and techniques are exemplified by case histories dealing with situations and problems pastoral counselors commonly meet. These case histories are based on real-life people and situations but details have been changed so as to protect the identity of the persons involved. In presenting each case, I have tried to portray the mental and emotional experience of the person in a particular situation, such as how a man feels when his wife has died or walked out on him, or a woman when she discovers that her teenage son is involved in drugs, and then give the research on how each of these persons can be helped. By using this procedure it is my hope that you will learn not only how to use the various skills and techniques but also how to deal with some of the problem situations commonly seen in pastoral counseling.

2

Counseling in Pastoral Ministry

The word counseling has a variety of meanings which range from giving advice to psychotherapy.[1] In popular usage, counseling often means giving advice to someone who is faced with some kind of a difficulty. For example, lawyers are said to counsel when they tell clients their legal rights and what they should do when they have been injured in an automobile accident; social workers when they counsel people how they should care for an aged senile parent; and career counselors when they counsel students who are about to graduate and need to decide on their future occupation. In all these cases, the common denominator seems to be giving advice or suggesting what a person should do.

In this book, the meaning of counseling goes beyond giving advice or making suggestions. Counseling is seen as a dialogue in which a counselor establishes helping relationships with persons to help them better understand themselves and the situation in which they find themselves and then help them solve their problem, or offer emotional support if the problem cannot be solved. The focus of the counseling is on the person with a problem rather than the type of problem the person faces. Counseling aims at helping people help themselves. At times, it may include advice-giving, but the giving of advice is only one of many skills the counselor uses.

Counseling in pastoral ministry is a particular type of counseling which is distinguished from other types of counseling by the approach and orientation the counselor takes. Counselors in pastoral ministry hold and follow a set of Christian beliefs and values and usually their counselees hold and follow the same beliefs and values, which manifest themselves either directly or indirectly in the counseling process. The primary and explicit goal of counselors in pastoral ministry is to help Christians solve their problems in a way that follows the message of Jesus Christ as found in the Gospels and the teaching of the Church. Much of the counseling undertaken by pastoral counselors deals with some kind of a problem the counselee is facing. The problem is discussed in the context of the counselee's Christian faith and commitment which distinguishes counseling in pastoral ministry from other types of counseling. For example, when a counselor in pastoral ministry attempts to help someone with a marriage problem, the Christian view of marriage as a permanent commitment will inevitably come up. If the counselee talks of getting a divorce, the counselor will either directly or indirectly refer to the permanence and sanctity of the marriage commitment, which the counselor holds as a committed Christian and assumes that the Christian counselee also holds.

Counseling in pastoral ministry is built upon the understanding that one party is a helper while the other seeks help. The people who seek help assume that the counselor is a person of faith, trustworthy, knowledgeable and has had some experience in counseling, and consequently can help them. They also assume that the counselor will either directly or indirectly share his or her faith with them during the counseling session.

PASTORAL COUNSELING IS NOT
A PASTORAL CONVERSATION

Pastoral counseling is not the same as a pastoral visit to the home of a parishioner, a home for the aged or a hospital. What takes place during such a visit can best be described as a pastoral conversation in which someone representing the Church discusses with a person a topic of general interest to both parties, such as what is going on within the family of the person visited or some event that is taking place in the Church. The purpose of the dialogue is to indicate that the priest, minister, sister or lay person who represents the Church is interested in and has a concern for the person being visited, and in particular for his or her spiritual well-being. Occasionally the one representing the Church may want to move beyond the level of conversation and begin the process of counseling, if the topic of conversation calls for counseling and the environment affords sufficient privacy. The more usual procedure, however, is to invite the person to come to the parish or chaplain's office. At times priests, ministers, sisters and lay pastoral counselors may have to engage in counseling under conditions where privacy is lacking, such as in a two-bed hospital room or in a room in a home for the aged where several others are close by, but they should counsel under these circumstances only out of necessity.

NOT SPIRITUAL DIRECTION

Pastoral counseling is not the same as spiritual direction. The main purpose of spiritual direction is to help people grow in the life of the Spirit. Spiritual directors try to help directees understand more fully their relationships with God and how God, especially in the person of Jesus Christ, is working in their lives. They are primarily concerned with the way the person relates to God and others.[2] Like counseling, spiritual direction seems to have a variety of meanings. For some directors, spiritual direction means listening to what people have to say about their prayer and spiritual life and then teaching or guiding them; for others, direction is quite similar to non-directive counseling where the director reflects back what the directees say about their life with God and then helps these directees see how the Holy Spirit is leading them.[3] In the latter case, the director "contributes to the verification of the life of faith and the concrete forms it assumes by examining with the individual the divine operation of which he or she is conscious. Progressively the genuine tenor of the concrete forms will emerge. In this case the accent is placed on the origin and nature of the operation of grace, on the successive and alternate phases of the painful searching for God, and on the joyful discovery of him."[4]

NOT PSYCHOLOGICAL COUNSELING OR PSYCHOTHERAPY

Counselors in pastoral ministry are part of the helping professions but serve a different function than clinical psychologists and psychiatrists who have had extensive training and are licensed to engage in psychological counseling and psychotherapy. The chief function of pastoral counselors is to help "normal" people live more Christian lives and solve their problems on the basis of their faith and Christian commitment; psychologists and psychiatrists treat people who are mentally and emotionally ill through the use of medical and psychological strategies. The chief function of psychiatrists and psychologists is to bring about a remission of psychological and physical symptoms, change in personality structure, and psychological growth. To accomplish all three, psychologists and psychiatrists use procedures and techniques not available to counselors in pastoral ministry. On occasion, however, some pastoral counselors may use one or other psychological technique which they have learned while attending a workshop or seminar on psychology or psychiatry. However, it should be noted that attendance at a workshop or even completing several courses does not equip pastoral counselors to undertake psychological counseling or psychotherapy. If pastoral counselors wish to engage in psychological counseling as well as pastoral counseling, they should have additional training and clinical experience, and then be licensed like other professionals.

NOT JUST GIVING ADVICE

As we noted before, some consider giving advice the essential component of counseling. Research, however, has shown that advice often has little effect on counselees and can at times even be harmful.[5] People are too complex to respond to stereotyped solutions. They may understand the advice but inner turmoil keeps them from really hearing and acting on it. At other times the reason why they are seeking help has little to do with facts and answers. When these people meet with what the counselor may consider sound advice, the advice really makes little impression on them because either they are not seeking advice or they are not yet ready to listen to advice.

NOT JUST AN ANALYSIS OF THE PROBLEM

Some people look upon counseling as an intellectual exercise. Counselors are experts at analyzing problems; they have the knack of sizing up the various elements of the problem, analyzing them and then presenting their analysis to the counselee. Good counselors are people who are insightful and skillfully explain to counselees the reasons why they think and act the way they do. Research has shown, however, that feelings and emotions play a major role in the counseling process; sometimes how we feel is as important as what we think.[6] A counselor can analyze the counselee's problem with the utmost clarity and the counselee can agree with the analysis but never use it because the analysis ignores how the person feels about the matter. People frequently can see on an intellectual level what they must do to solve a problem but the way they feel makes them incapable of putting into action what they see they should do. For example, a troubled father can usually see that he needs to exert firmer control over his fourteen year old delinquent son. Your telling him that he needs to be firmer in dealing with his son usually does not help him because he already knows this, or at least suspects it. This man's problem is rooted in something less evident, namely his own feelings of inadequacy as a parent, which makes him unable to deal with his rebellious son. Feelings and emotions often keep us from doing what we know we should do.

FAULTY COUNSELING HABITS

In comparison with other types of counselors, counselors in pastoral ministry often have limited formal training in counseling. Many pastoral counselors have developed a style of counseling through experience and have stayed with that style because they have found it effective. One of the aims of this book is to build upon what you as a counselor have already developed and then also help you eliminate any faulty habits that may lessen your effectiveness.

Usually faulty habits come from the overuse or incorrect

use of a counseling skill. For instance, some counselors rely too much on asking questions or give too much advice. While there are times when advice helps people, advice should be used sparingly, especially in the beginning phase of counseling.

Some counselors offer advice from their own frame of reference. They advise the counselee on the basis of what they would do if they were in the counselee's situation. This kind of advice may make little sense to the counselee because the counselee does not look at the situation the same way as the counselor.

Poor timing is another reason why advice fails to help the counselee. The advice is premature. The counselee is not ready to listen to the advice or pay the cost of following it.

How do you know when the advice you have given is helpful or will go unheeded? If the counselees make no comment when you give the advice, the odds favor their not using the advice. If the counselee uses the "Yes but" game, you know that the counselee has rejected your advice—for example, when you suggest that a man take his wife out to dinner to talk over an argument they had, he responds to your suggestion with "Yes but I have taken her out before and it only made matters worse," and then when you suggest that he might take her for a drive up the coast some evening, he replies with "Yes but my wife doesn't like to go on drives at night." Everything you suggest meets with a "Yes but." The counselee seems to have an endless list of reasons why everything you suggest will not work.

Another person may agree with what you suggest and respond with "You are so right; I must do that" but you know from the tone of the person's voice that she has no intention of following what you have advised.

Psychotherapists sometimes speak of the "lightbulb" experience. When the counselor suggests a solution to a problem, the counselee's face lights up and he or she exclaims: "That's great. Why didn't I think of that?" You know then that the counselee has accepted your suggestion or advice and will probably use it.

We are each responsible for our own actions. The counselor's giving advice takes this responsibility away from the person and places it on the counselor's shoulders. The excessive use of advice can actually harm counselees because it deprives them of the opportunity to learn how to take responsibility for themselves and may cause them to become overly dependent on the counselor. Finally, if the advice does not work out, people tend to blame the counselor. If the advice fails several times, they may lose trust in the counselor, or even the whole process of counseling.

AN EXAMPLE OF TWO APPROACHES

The following is an example of two different approaches to the same person with a problem: one counselor relies on advice and suggestions while the other tries to understand what the counselee is experiencing and then reflects this understanding to the counselee.

Mrs. Smith has just been abandoned by her husband after ten years of marriage. From the beginning the marriage has been unstable. She and her husband have had periodic violent arguments, and on several occasions he has stormed out of the house, only to return three or four days later. Greatly distressed, Mrs. Smith seeks help from her pastor. Ostensibly she indicates that she wants nothing more than advice. Should she begin to make arrangements for the care of the children and then find a job? Should she start divorce proceedings and demand that her husband support the children? If he comes back, should she take him back just as she has done before? After listening to Mrs. Smith's account, the pastor focuses his attention on the instability of the marriage and its effect on the children. He speaks of the obligation to provide an atmosphere where the children can grow up good, Christian people. He then suggests some specific arrangements for the support of the children. He advises her to consult a lawyer about the best way to make her husband contribute to their support. Mrs. Smith balks at the advice and offers many superficial objections. The pastor tries to convince Mrs. Smith that she must face the reality of her situation. The interview ends with both parties being dissatisfied.

As Mrs. Smith becomes even more distraught, a friend recommends that she consult with a priest who has had training in counseling psychology. The priest immediately recognizes Mrs. Smith's emotional turmoil and concludes that any attempt at getting her to make decisions would be useless. He becomes an attentive, interested listener. For more than an hour Mrs. Smith pours out her hostility and anger toward her husband and indicates that she feels confined as the mother of four small children. The priest encourages her to release her pent-up feelings and occasionally by means of well-formulated comments or questions shows that he understands how she feels. Toward the end of the hour she begins to realize that in some way she is contributing to her marital problem and emotional condition. She finishes by saying that she feels much better and wants to come back again. Four days later she returns and announces that her husband has returned. She says that even under the most trying circumstances they have been able to talk to each other; they have discussed their latest argument and have decided that they both were at fault. She then asks if the counselor would be willing to see the two of them, as they think they both need help if the marriage is to be saved.

COUNSELING ORIENTATIONS

Counselors in pastoral ministry may approach their task from any of three orientations: (1) as an expert, (2) as an interested and understanding helper, and (3) as a facilitator in the process of problem-solving. All three have a place in pastoral counseling but no one approach is appropriate for every situation. Each approach presupposes attentive listening so the counselor can understand what the individual is experiencing, what he or she is seeking from counseling, and what can be done to improve the situation.

THE EXPERT

For centuries, priests and ministers have served as experts in religion. When anyone had a problem involving not only faith and theology but also daily living, he or she would consult a priest or minister. A hundred years ago there were no psychiatrists or psychologists; thirty years ago both of these professions were highly suspect. If a person needed to talk over a personal matter or problem with another, the most logical and available person was the parish priest or minister. Because of his unique education in philosophy and theology the parish priest or minister was considered a generalized expert. He could answer people's questions not only about religion but also about most any other matter and then advise the person what he or she should do. Much of the advice that priests or ministers gave was based on their own past experience in helping people and common sense.

Today people still need the theological expertise of the priest or minister. They need information about their faith; they particularly need information about morality and Christian values. The following incident is an example of a priest who served as an expert consultant and counselor.

A well-known member of a parish comes to his pastor to talk about the disintegration of his marriage. He tells of a union that is a marriage in name only. He says that he and his wife have been emotionally alienated for years. Violent arguments followed by periods of neither speaking to the other have marked the marriage almost from the beginning. The only bond tying them together has been the raising of four children who are now grown and out of the home. Three years ago and after twenty-five years of marriage, he and his wife had marriage counseling from a psychologist for a period of three months but with little success. The parishioner says he attends daily Mass; his faith means a great deal to him since it gives him the strength to face his difficult life. On the other hand, his wife who is a convert to Catholicism no longer goes to church. She finds her husband's pious practices annoying. She told him that she wants a divorce. The parishioner says that he is very concerned about his status in the Catholic Church if he accedes to his wife's wishes. He is under the impression that being divorced means an end to active membership in the Church and his right to receive the sacraments. He says he would rather struggle along married than give up his Catholic faith.

What this man needs is some correct information about the position of the Church on divorce. He needs to know how a divorced person stands in the eyes of the Church, what he can do and what he cannot do. He may also need emotional support, once he decides what is the best course to take. He does not need counseling as much as he needs information from an expert in moral theology and canon law.

THE UNDERSTANDING HELPER

Many people need more than information and answers; they need the assistance of an understanding person. Carl Rogers has spent his life studying what it means to be an understanding person.[8] Rogers began his career as a psychologist in the psychoanalytic tradition. As he progressed, he became increasingly disillusioned with the psychoanalytic method. Gradually he came to realize the importance of the client's subjective experience. Rogers found that if two conditions were present, the client usually improved: (1) when the counselor was able to show positive regard for the client, not judging the client and accepting the client as a person without placing any preconceived conditions for acceptance, and (2) when the counselor showed empathetic understanding of the client.

Rogers described empathetic understanding as a way of being with another person. "It means entering the private perceptual world of the other and becoming thoroughly at home with it. It involves being sensitive, moment by moment, to the changing felt meanings which flow in this other person, to fear or rage or tenderness or confusion or whatever he or she is experiencing. It means temporarily living in the other's life moving about in it without making judgments; it means sensing meanings of which he or she is scarcely aware, but not trying to uncover totally unconscious feelings, since this would be too threatening. It includes your sensing of the person's world as you look with fresh, unfrightened eyes at elements of which he or she is fearful. It means frequently checking with the person as to the accuracy of your sensings, and being guided by the response you receive. You are a confident companion to the person in his or her inner world."[9]

As you listen to a counselee, you should ask yourself: What is this person experiencing? What is going on in this person's life that he or she is trying to convey to me? How does he or she feel about it? What words will best describe the counselee's inner experience for the counselee?[10]

Empathetic communication causes counselees to look at themselves and discover aspects of themselves and the situation in which they find themselves that they had not seen before, to replace old destructive views of themselves with new positive ones, and to move toward a solution of their problem, if there is a problem. A good part of the progress is due to the realization that one is no longer alone on life's journey but is accompanied by an understanding companion. Rogers found that the very experience of being understood and unconditionally accepted by another human being causes people to be more positive in the way they view themselves, and, as a consequence, to make better use of their talents and abilities in facing whatever problem disturbs them.[11]

Many people who seek pastoral counseling are not looking for answers and solutions; they are simply looking for understanding and support in a period of great need; with time they feel they will be able to resolve their difficulty. Others come already knowing the answer to their problem; they want to "bounce it off" a trusted and reliable person. Still others are seeking a solution to their problem but they do not want you to take over their lives and give them the solution to their problem. They want you to help them to decide what they should do but they do not want you to make the final decision. These people are convinced that they can make their own decisions if they have the opportunity to talk it over with a trustworthy person. In all three of the above-mentioned situations, the person-centered approach of Carl Rogers can be most helpful, provided the counselee is articulate, is moderately aware of his or her own feelings, and has the inner strength to make a decision.

FACILITATING THE PROBLEM-SOLVING PROCESS

Finally the counselor in pastoral ministry may act as a facilitator in the process of problem-solving. In this approach the counselor tries to help people find solutions to problems they face.[12] The counselor's function is to facilitate the process; it is not to solve the problem for the person by giving advice. The counselor simply sets up a framework which assists the person in arriving at a workable solution.

To start the process you need to listen attentively to what the person has to say about the difficulty he or she is experiencing and then try to understand it from that person's point of view. You should be interested in how the person feels about the matter and what it means to him or her, since we each have our own way of looking at a situation. What is devastating for one person is a minor obstacle for another. Then you should summarize what the counselee has told you about the problem or difficulty and check for the accuracy of your summary. The counselee is now in a position to consider possible solutions to his or her problem. After considering what options he or she may have, you urge the counselee to review each option and list what favors and what is against each option. The counselee is then asked to weigh and compare the options and finally decide on the option he or she thinks is most likely to succeed. Once the counselee decides which option looks the best, you try to get him or her to consider ways of implementing the option. The description of the problem-solving process given above is merely a summary; we shall consider this process in greater detail in a later chapter.

SUMMARY

Counseling in pastoral ministry is a dialogue in which a counselor establishes a helping relationship and attempts to assist another in bringing about changes in his or her way of living, solving a problem or simply feeling supported by a caring person who represents the Church, all of which is done in the context of the individual's Christian faith and values. The counselor may function as (1) an expert, (2) an understanding helper, and/or (3) a facilitator in the problem-solving process. The process of counseling may call for the use of all three or just one or other of these functions. Excessive advice-giving is a common fault among some counselors in pastoral ministry. While there are times when advice is called for, advice often goes unheeded, makes the person dependent on the counselor, and may hinder the counselee's growth as a Christian person.

3

Christian Faith and Values

Faith and values distinguish pastoral counseling from other forms of counseling. In Christian pastoral counseling the counselor and the counselee profess a belief in Christianity and follow a Christian way of living. Counselors in pastoral ministry are called to be counselors because of their faith and commitment to Christian values, and this faith and commitment should, therefore, play a major role in their counseling. Usually people who seek pastoral counseling expect that what they believe will in some way enter into the counseling process. The topic the counselee wishes to discuss may deal directly with matters of religion and/or Christian values, in which case the counselor makes use of his or her faith to help the counselee, or it may be a matter the counselee sees as having little connection with religion. In this case, the task of the pastoral counselor is to link the topic under discussion to the faith and values of the counselee. In some way both the counselor's and the counselee's faith and values should play a part in the counseling process, even though there may seem to be little or no connection between what the person wants to discuss and his or her religious convictions.

FAITH

When we hear the word "faith," the first thing that usually comes to mind is a set of beliefs like those found in the Nicene or Apostles' Creed. We think of the act of faith whereby we give assent to a statement in one of these Creeds, such as "We believe in one God, the Father, the Almighty, maker of heaven and earth." The First Vatican Council defines faith in the following manner: "Faith is a supernatural virtue by which, guided and aided by grace, we hold as true what God has revealed, not because we have perceived its intrinsic truth by our own reason but because of the authority of God who can neither deceive nor be deceived." (Session III, cap. 3) Thus faith is a lasting state of mind which allows us to accept the truths God has revealed to us about himself and his plans for the world.[1] What God has revealed is set but what a particular revealed truth means to an individual can differ from one person to another. We assent to the statement "We believe in one God, the Father, the Almighty" because we accept it as a revealed truth. The statement itself is constant but what the statement means to a person varies from individual to individual. As a consequence of development, learning and experience, we each have a somewhat different way of looking at God and the content of our faith.[2] God means something different to a child or teenager than he does to an adult. As we grow older, hopefully our understanding of who God is becomes more mature. What changes is not the statement "We believe in God, the Father, the Almighty" but what the statement means to us. In relating faith to counseling, we shall focus on what faith means to the individual and what part it plays in his or her everyday life. We do not mean to imply, however, that pastoral counselors never deal with the act of faith. Sometimes several counseling sessions may need to be devoted to helping counselees clarify what they believe.

DIFFERENCES IN COMMITMENT

Within both the Catholic and Protestant traditions, the faith of individual Christians differs widely. Some people are totally committed to Jesus Christ and what he taught while others say they are Christians but Christianity is simply a formality that has little to do with their lives. Between these two extremes are many levels of commitment. It is important that you understand what God and what Jesus Christ taught means to your counselee and the extent of his or her commitment. This understanding allows you to determine whether and to what extent you can make use of the counselee's faith as a motivating factor. Before you can use people's faith as a motivator, you may have to help them clarify what they believe, and at times you may even have to instruct them about some of the beliefs the Church teaches.

In its fullness, "Christian faith is an encounter with Jesus Christ, who meets the believer through his Spirit, while the believer meets Jesus Christ through the gift of faith, which allows the believer to know and accept Christ and the message Christ taught. It is an enduring state of the total person that involves knowledge, experience, trust, feelings and emotions, and commitment."[3] It is this faith-relationship with Jesus Christ that the counselor in pastoral ministry should try to understand and use in the counseling process.

OPENNESS TO GOD

The basic message that Jesus Christ taught is that God is Father, Son and Holy Spirit and as Christians we are called to relate to this Triune God. Relating to God means listening to God when he speaks to us. God speaks to us in various ways. God speaks to us through his revealed word as manifested in the Old and New Testament. He also speaks through the Church and its ministers. He speaks through others and through the seemingly ordinary events of life. Finally, he speaks to us through the Holy Spirit. People of faith can listen to the voice of God as it comes to them from these sources.

Some people, however, read the Scriptures or listen to them but gain little or no insight from them. They regard Scripture as just another piece of literature. Although they have been exposed to the word of God, they do not hear it. Others hear the message of the Gospel proclaimed by the ministers of the Church but what they hear fails to have any personal meaning. Still others are oblivious of God speaking to them through a husband or wife, a friend, or even an enemy. The message goes unheeded because they do not recognize that it comes from God. And, finally, the Spirit speaks directly to some people urging them to think and act in a certain way, but the inspiration is lost on them because they are too distracted by inner turmoil to listen to anything else. One of the functions of counseling in pastoral ministry is to prepare the individual to listen to the voice of God when he speaks.

This approach to counseling plays down active intervention on the part of the counselor and stresses the action of God in helping people handle their difficulties. The counselor acts as a facilitator rather than an activator. The main function of the counselor is to prepare the way for the Spirit. As St. Paul put it, "I planted, Apollos watered, but God has given the growth" (1 Cor 3:6). The counselor in pastoral ministry realizes that growth and healing are fruits of the Spirit; the counselor's task is simply to dispose the person to respond to the voice of God. On the basis of revelation, it is assumed that if people are properly disposed and pray for help, God will help them overcome the difficulty whatever it may be or give them the strength to live with it (Mt 7:7).

OBSTACLES TO LISTENING TO GOD

There are several obstacles that keep people from listening to God: rejection of the Spirit, sin, and inner turmoil. The first obstacle is found in those who have been exposed to Christianity and offered the gift of faith, but either have refused to accept it or, once having accepted it, have later rejected it. It is the function of the counselor to help these people see that they have rejected the Spirit, find the reasons for the rejection, and, if possible, help them to listen to and follow the Spirit once again.

The second obstacle, sin, is found in those who retain their belief in God but choose their own will in preference to his. They turn their backs on God and as a consequence frequently do not hear the Spirit when it speaks to them. Repeated sin weakens faith so that it gradually becomes less and less meaningful. One goal of counseling in pastoral ministry is to bring about a reconciliation with God, which turns sinners from sin and makes them open to the voice of God.

The third obstacle, inner turmoil, affects those whose inner conflicts and frustrations are so intense that they no longer possess peace of mind. Fear, anxiety, hostility, and guilt demand most of their attention. There is such an uproar within that the voice of God cannot penetrate their awarenesses. If the individual is not seriously disturbed, you as a counselor may help the individual regain inner peace by your empathetic listening; if the individual is seriously disturbed, referral to a psychiatrist or psychologist may be in order.

OPENNESS TO SELF

Openness to God depends upon openness to self. We use self-awareness as a stepping-stone to God. People who surround themselves with protective devices cannot see God working in their world. Self-understanding and self-acceptance are closely linked to accepting the word of God. Openness to self prepares the ground for an awareness of the Spirit "who breathes where he will."

Baute says that "pastoral counseling can be described as an interpersonal relationship of acceptance, understanding, and communication between priest (or clergyman) and a parishioner for the purpose of assisting that person in making choices and decisions, and thus pursue his own Christian vocation according to his capacities with more happiness."[4] These choices and decisions can be made on the basis of God speaking to the individual.

Openness to the voice of God implies not a loss of freedom but increased freedom. The purpose of counseling in pastoral ministry is to create within individuals freedom to make decisions on the basis of their faith, as these are informed by the Spirit, and not on the basis of compulsions, fear, guilt, or hostility. The communicated acceptance and understanding of the counselor permits counselees to realize the freedom they need to listen to God as he speaks to them. The counselor works at establishing an atmosphere as free as possible from fear and anxiety, one which allows counselees to look at themselves as they actually are.

St. Paul in his Letter to the Galatians describes how one can determine whether an individual is acting freely according to the promptings of the Spirit. "But the fruit of the Spirit is love, joy, peace, patience, kindness, goodness, faithfulness, gentleness, and self-control" (Gal 5:22). Spiritual writers have dealt at length with the discernment of the spirits. Among the many signs that God is actually moving the individual are a sincere, continuing desire to imitate Christ, truthfulness and honesty, openness to counsel, flexibility of will, serenity, and humility.[5] These characteristics are signs that the counselee is open to the inspiration of the Spirit.

CHRISTIAN VALUES

Christian values stem from faith. A value is "that which is esteemed, prized, or deemed worthwhile and desirable by a person or culture."[6] Faith in Jesus Christ and the message he taught causes us to look upon certain ways of thinking, acting, and living as worthwhile and desirable; these special ways of thinking, acting, and living constitute a system of Christian values. An example of a Christian value is respect for the human dignity of each person with whom we come in contact, which stems from the commandment Jesus Christ gave us to love our neighbor as ourselves. This Christian value determines how we think, feel and act in regard to other people, races and nations, even those we may not like or may consider enemies. We prize all other human beings because of their dignity as creatures of God and because both we and they have God as a common Father. This respect and love for others is closely linked to the commandment to "love God with all your heart, with all your soul and with all your mind" (Mt 22:37). The two commandments are as one and the foundation for all our Christian values.

In the Sermon on the Mount Jesus taught a number of mental states or conditions that are to be prized and valued by all Christians: (Matthew, 5, 3–12)

Blessed are the poor in spirit, for theirs is the kingdom of heaven.

Blessed are those who mourn, for they shall be comforted.

Blessed are the meek, for they shall inherit the earth.

Blessed are those who hunger and thirst for righteousness, for they shall be satisfied.

Blessed are the merciful, they shall receive mercy.

Blessed are the pure in heart, they shall see God.

Blessed are the peacemakers, for they shall be called sons of God.

Blessed are those who are persecuted for righteousness' sake, for theirs is the kingdom of heaven (Mt. 5:3–12).

Each of these statements contains a value which those who follow the Christian way of life are exhorted to follow.

PLACE OF VALUES IN COUNSELING

Just as in the case of faith, Christian counselors consciously or unconsciously manifest their values when they counsel.[7] Sometimes the counselor may deal directly with a value, as in the case of the counselor who tries to help a pregnant sixteen year old who is contemplating having an abortion and needs to reflect upon the value of human life, even in its fetal stage, or the husband who has become sexually involved with his secretary and needs to consider the value he places on his marriage, wife and children; at other times, the counselor's values may manifest themselves only indirectly, as in the case of a priest-counselor who is attempting to understand and help a young man who wants to transfer from a Catholic university to a state university or a nun-counselor who is trying to help a young woman who says she wants to leave her religious community, even though she is not clear why she wants to leave it. In these latter two cases, the values the one counselor places on a Catholic education and the other on a religious vocation will most probably manifest themselves, even though the counselors may make every effort to appear neutral so as to allow the two young people to make their own decisions after considering all the factors involved in the decision.

MODELING FAITH AND VALUES

Psychologists speak of a process called modeling. The term "modeling" refers to the "process of observational learning in which the behavior of an individual or a group—the model—acts as a stimulus for similar thoughts, attitudes and behaviors on the part of another individual who observes the model's performance."[8] In other words, the person imitates the behavior of a model. In pastoral counseling the counselee imitates the faith and Christian values of the counselor. Counselors in pastoral ministry become models by the very fact that they are esteemed by the counselees.[9] Any overt or covert manifestation of the counselor's faith or values makes an impression on the counselee and he or she is apt to imitate what the pastoral counselor believes and practices.

During a counseling session some pastoral counselors pray with the person they are counseling. Praying with a person has a twofold benefit: it calls upon God's help for the enterprise and it serves as a model of prayer for the counselee. The counselor who is a person of faith and aware of God's presence in his or her life is quite likely to inspire a similar awareness in the counselee. If the counselor manifests an open trust in God's providence, the counselee is apt to be influenced by this trust and develop a similar trust. To be effective as a pastoral counselor you need to be a person of faith; it is not enough to be just well trained in psychological skills and techniques.

Research shows that "a model who is similar to the observer in sex, age, race and attitude is more likely to be imitated than a dissimilar model. With similarity, the observer is assured that the behaviors shown are appropriate and attainable by someone like himself. Models who possess prestige in the eyes of the observer are generally more likely to be imitated than low prestige models. It is important, however, to avoid models whose status level is so prestigious that the observer sees their behavior as an unrealistic guide for his behavior. Probably the best choice of a model in this regard is someone who is just one or two steps advanced from the position of an observer, or one who proceeds from a position of relative similarity to the observer to one of greater proficiency."[10] This research indicates that the counselor in pastoral ministry should be a person of greater faith and commitment than the individual being counseled but at the same time not so advanced on the road to holiness as to be beyond the counselee's reach. Generally speaking, men counselors will be more effective as models with men, and women counselors with women.[11] The closer the ages of the counselor and the counselee, the more likely modeling will take place.

FAITH SHARING

Faith sharing is another tool at the disposal of counselors in pastoral ministry. In faith sharing counselors reveal their faith and Christian values to the people they are counseling. Jourard has shown that counselors who talk about their feelings and background facilitate a similar disclosure by the counselee.[12] When you are willing to talk openly about what you believe and esteem you will find not only that counselees gain some new understanding of their own faith and values but that they are more willing to talk about what they believe and how it influences their lives. Sharing your faith experiences with others lessens the counselee's reluctance to talk about what he or she believes and causes the counselee to examine the depth of his or her own commitment. It also produces a bond of unity between the counselor and the counselee. Faith sharing on the part of the counselor can be a powerful means to bring about change in the counselee's faith.

SUMMARY

Faith and values distinguish counseling in pastoral ministry from all other forms of counseling. Both the counselor and the counselee manifest what they believe and what they prize and esteem as worthwhile during almost every counseling session. Often faith and Christian values are the topic of the dialogue, but even when neither faith nor values are openly discussed, they often enter the process indirectly. It is the task of the pastoral counselor to link both faith and Christian values to the matter the counselee is discussing, when counselees see little connection between their problem and their religion.

Because of their position in the Church, counselors in pastoral ministry act either directly or indirectly as models for people who come to them for counseling, which means that the counselor should be a person of strong faith and committed to Christian values. A way of strengthening the faith of counselees is for counselors to share their faith with their counselees. When counselors pray with counselees they share their faith in God with the counselees and give them a model of how they should pray. Faith can be a powerful motivating factor in urging people to take the steps needed to solve a problem.

Values are those things in our lives that we esteem and prize as important. Christian values flow from the teaching of Jesus Christ and motivate us to think, act and relate with others in a distinctive manner. Christian counselors in pastoral ministry should be fully committed to the values taught by Jesus Christ which they either openly or indirectly impart to those who come to them for help.

4

Feelings and Emotions

Feelings and emotions play an important but often unnoticed role in the average person's daily life. For example, an employee with six children makes an error in judgment which costs the firm several thousand dollars. He is reprehended and told that a similar mistake will mean the end of his job. As a result he begins to experience feelings of guilt and fear which make him feel less confident on the job and edgy, restless and ill at ease at home. His friends notice that he is quieter and more reserved. Detecting a change in himself, particularly in his relationship with his wife, he approaches a counselor at his local parish. He is vague about his reason for coming, and tells of a disagreement with his wife over the disciplining of a teenage son. The source of the trouble, however, lies in his inability to recognize how his life is being disrupted by feelings of guilt and fear and then cope with these feelings.

Most of us realize that we have feelings and emotions, but when asked to define these we are at a loss. We have all felt happy or sad; we have all shared joy and love with others; we have all become angry and fearful. These are common inner experiences which color our contacts with people and things. Allport has defined emotions as "stirred up conditions of the

43

organism."[1] They act as instigators, helping us to get what we need to survive and grow as people. At times they are danger signals telling us that something is wrong and that we had better alter our course of action. They constitute that part of mental functioning which psychologists call affective. The affect refers to feelings and emotions as opposed to thinking and willing. Because theology places the emphasis on knowledge and responsibility, pastoral counselors are sometimes prone to overlook the affective side of the mind.

FEELINGS

Affective reactions are frequently separated into two types, feelings and emotions. Feelings can be defined as positive or negative reactions to an experience.[2] They usually result from something that we like or dislike, and they are less intense than emotions such as fear, anger, or jealousy. When one has a positive affective reaction, the person experiences pleasure. For example, at breakfast a man may find a cup of coffee pleasant but while waiting for his wife to fix it, he experiences a negative, unpleasant reaction.

EMOTIONS

Emotions are more profound, pervasive, and intense than feelings.[3] There is, however, no sharp line of demarcation between these two states. One distinction between them is that an emotion is generally attached to a definite object or class of objects. Some people are afraid of dogs or riding in an elevator. Others are angry with a spouse or employer. These objects cause the emotional reaction, even though they may not be aware of the connection.

To be empathetic, it is necessary to understand a person's emotional reactions; such understanding requires some knowledge of how feelings and emotions work. One of the more obvious qualities is spontaneity.[4] In a terrifying situation we automatically experience fear. The soldier who is pinned down in a cross-fire is afraid, though he may try to repress or rationalize away his fear. The soldier appraises the extreme danger in which he finds himself and immediately undergoes an emotional response. He can control his actions but he cannot turn off the emotional reaction. A common misconception is that if we have character we should have complete control over our feelings and emotions; we should be able to turn them off and on at will. Actually fear, anger, jealousy and guilt are spontaneous reactions which cannot be controlled by will power, once we become aware of the object that stimulates them. Hence we are not responsible for such emotions. The guilt-ridden husband who has cheated on his wife whom he loves does not choose to feel guilty nor can he free himself from guilt through an act of the will. He can control the sinful act but not the affective response.

FUNCTIONS OF FEAR AND GUILT

Emotions like fear, anger and guilt can be either helpful or harmful. Since the experience of guilt is painful, the desire to avoid it often motivates people to follow their moral code; if the temptation is too strong and they do violate the code, their guilt prompts sorrow, amendment, and reparation. When guilt feelings are not relieved they continue to build up and can lead to "acting out," as in the case of the alcoholic who continues his compulsive drinking to escape his guilt.

Guilt is similar to fear in many ways. We might even call it moral fear. Fear is often an extremely useful experience, as it warns us to stay away from danger. If we were completely fearless, we would have trouble staying alive. Virtually every emotion can, under certain circumstances, have a beneficial effect, if it prompts us to protect or develop ourselves either physically or psychologically.

THE APPRAISAL

An emotional response involves an appraisal. People who are afraid of snakes appraise them as potentially dangerous. When they see a snake in the field, they automatically evaluate it as a thing to be avoided.

Many of our emotions are learned from either personal experience or contact with others. The woman who has been bitten learns to fear snakes as a result of her unfortunate experience. The child feels guilty for stealing his friend's baseball because he has been taught that stealing is wrong. Since each individual has a different set of learning experiences, his or her emotional reactions are unique.[5] Counselors should grasp as best they can the nature of the counselee's emotional experience. Emotional responses form an important part of the counselee's frame of reference. Thus, one boy may be overcome with guilt and shame when he steals, whereas another child may shrug off his deed as inconsequential. In helping either child, counselors should concentrate on the particular emotional reaction.

There is a connection between emotion and intelligence. Brighter people tend to have a more complex emotional life, and thus they are more difficult to understand. "This fact suggests that emotional disturbance is like a temporary breakdown in a piece of machinery or electrical equipment; the more complex the equipment, the greater number of things by which the operation may be disturbed, the greater the aberration from normal function may be and the longer it may take to get it back in working order."[6]

Emotions follow a developmental sequence like any other component of the human organism.[7] As children grow, their bodies grow and take on a more mature contour; similarly their emotions take on more mature patterns of expression. The emotional reactions of a small child are short-lived; those of an adolescent and adult are more prolonged. The emotional outbursts of a small child may seem quite violent but are actually shallow. A trivial frustration may evoke a tantrum, but five minutes later the child has forgotten the incident. An adult's response lasts longer and usually requires a more significant cause.

Emotional immaturity is a failure on the part of adolescents or adults to outgrow some of their emotional patterns. They still have certain reactions of anger or fear which are similar to what they had when they were four or five years old. For example, an adolescent may become excessively angry when contradicted and respond with a childish outburst. In happy circumstances he is momentarily overcome with euphoria, but his or her experience has little depth or duration.

HANDLING EMOTIONS

An emotional experience can be handled in several different ways. It can be expressed openly, channeled, suppressed or repressed. Some people develop the habit of constantly expressing their emotions. They wear their hearts on their sleeves. They are effusive and demonstrative. Others do not seem to have an emotion in their bodies. They may be experiencing the same emotions as the first group, but they do not show their feelings. Both types of response have their limitations. Individuals who constantly express their feelings may often find themselves at odds with others. Flying off the handle and bursting into tears is unacceptable behavior in most cultures. Rage, a violent form of anger accompanied by actual attack, elicits either disapproval or a similar rage—and perhaps a fight—from the other person.

When we are unable to express our emotions or think it unwise to do so, we can either channel or inhibit them. Channeling involves acknowledging our emotions and choosing some indirect means of expressing them. For instance, a woman may become angry with her husband, but instead of attacking him verbally or even physically, she goes out and jogs.

There are occasions, however, when we can neither express nor channel our emotions and must either suppress or repress them. Suppression implies a voluntary attempt to put aside the emotion, repression an involuntary blocking of the emotion from consciousness. In suppression, individuals determine that they are going to stop thinking angry thoughts. Each time hateful thoughts return to their minds, they actively try to banish them. In the case of repression, people do not even know that they are angry or at least do not realize how angry they are. They may feel vaguely uncomfortable, but they do not realize why they are experiencing the hostility. Of all the methods of handling feelings and emotions, repression can be the most destructive. Repressed feelings are dangerous to both physical and psychological equilibrium. Sometimes anger may suddenly crop up in an unfounded attack on a bystander, and the angry person will be at a loss to explain his or her actions. A most important requisite in coping with one's emotions is to acknowledge and accept them. Once people acknowledge to themselves that they are angry at an individual or situation, they can begin to control their actions. If they experience vague feelings of frustration and hostility, they cannot cope with themselves or the situation. Sometimes by talking things over with another person, like a counselor, they can see how they really feel and can deal with the cause of their emotions.

FEELINGS AND MOTIVATION

A major effect of feelings and emotions is motivation. Frequently we do something because it is pleasant or refuse to do it because it is unpleasant. Our feelings provide the driving force behind our activity. Without our feelings and emotions we would probably become stagnant. We would have little incentive to undertake the difficult or to avoid the harmful. Feelings are often the main cause for a person seeking counseling or psychotherapy. People feel anxious about the deterioration of their marriages or they are depressed about the lack of meaning in their lives. It is unlikely that intellectual convictions alone would make them seek help from a counselor; their distressing emotions provide the strongest impetus. Emotional distress usually also motivates the severely neurotic person to begin counseling and psychotherapy and to continue through many painful hours of therapy to completion. We all find it difficult to live with distressing emotions like fear, anger, jealousy and anxiety, and we all look for means of escape. Counselors and psychotherapists utilize this human characteristic in their dealings with individuals.

EMOTIONAL ABREACTION

One function of counseling is to effect an abreaction. This term signifies a release or weakening of emotional tension caused by conflict or repression. In the non-threatening atmosphere of counseling, people are able to speak freely about how they feel. Talking about their anger or fear lessens their distress and makes them more relaxed. The process of talking brings about the abreaction. It is often necessary not only to express emotions and feelings but also to appraise the source and circumstances of the reaction.[8] When counselees can see that there are other, better responses to their situation, they can usually put aside their anger. Better control and greater ability to make rational decisions often result from the abreaction.

ANXIETY

There are four affective reactions that are most frequently encountered in pastoral counseling: anxiety, hostility, guilt and grief. Anxiety is a part of everyone's life. It is more a feeling than an emotion. It ranges from a mild motivating force to a severely painful experience. Anxiety is a state of apprehension, concern and uneasiness, closely related to fear.[9] It is distinguished from fear by its vagueness and lack of a definite object. When people are anxious, they are concerned about an undefined future danger. They are apprehensive that something awful may happen but they are not sure what. This unpleasant state frequently prompts some to seek an escape or to seek help from a counselor.

Anxiety is often accompanied by worry. The anxious person wonders, "What is going to happen to me?" and worries, "What will I do when . . . ?" Counselors need not be in business very long before they come across the person who is worried about a multitude of things, some significant and others inconsequential. A woman may be apprehensive about her husband's health (which is average for a man of forty-five), her job (where she has received a raise every year for the past five years), the loss of a friend (who was not a close friend anyway), arriving late for an appointment and a host of other concerns expressed during a single half-hour. Such an individual is probably experiencing a high level of anxiety, which she attaches to almost every convenient object. To understand what this person is experiencing it is necessary to keep in mind that she is a highly anxious person who really does not know what is causing her anxiety.

Anxiety, like any other affective response, can be beneficial as well as destructive. Experienced speakers often know that they are most effective when they feel somewhat anxious. A mild level of anxiety sharpens one's capabilities and leads to a better performance. Even daily living can bring a certain amount of anxiety. We are all vaguely apprehensive about failing or getting into an accident. Only when anxiety exceeds the normal level does it become an handicap.

"Normal anxiety is proportionate to the objective danger and is relieved when the threat is removed while neurotic anxiety is enduring and disproportionate."[10] Neurotic anxiety can become so extreme that it disrupts normal functioning. Neurotics may find that their thinking, reasoning, and concentration are impaired. They may be restless and irritable, and may even reach the stage when they feel that they are "falling apart." Obviously such persons need more care than the counselor in pastoral ministry can provide.

HOSTILITY AND ANGER

Hostility is another affective reaction encountered in pastoral counseling. Like anxiety it is vague and can be better described as a feeling than as an emotion. It is not easy to perceive anxiety, since many of its manifestations are disguised. Hostility is a vague expression of anger in the form of sarcastic, belittling, hypercritical or nagging remarks. Often neither the counselor nor the counselee realizes the extent of the counselee's hostility and its effect on his or her capacity to deal with a problem.

Hostility is often the result of frustration and dissatisfaction with one's life.[11] People who do not get what they think they should from life may get angry without being conscious of the full impact of their anger. Instead, they have a mild feeling of discontent, frustration and depression. Often the source of the reaction is discontent with oneself, although hostility can also result from being frustrated by other people or by external circumstances.

Like other feelings and emotions, hostility and anger have a constructive purpose. They give us motivation and stamina to accomplish a difficult task. Only when these feelings go unrecognized do they become disproportionate and hinder normal functioning.

Both anger and hostility may produce a similar reaction in the person toward whom they are directed. Unless counselors are conscious of the counselee's hostility toward them, they may, in turn, experience hostility toward the counselee. When they see signs of hostility in the counselee, they should realize that this hostility is probably not directed at them personally but is instead an instance of general hostility directed at them as the immediate target. If counselors interpret this emotion as a personal attack on themselves, they will probably react with anger and damage their working relationship with the counselee.

GUILT

Since religion is closely tied to morality, counselors in pastoral ministry frequently encounter the emotion of guilt. "The feeling of guilt may be described as a painful emotion, such as a sense of unworthiness relating to the realization of an over-wide discrepancy between one's own conduct and the moral and ethical code one has set up for himself. As such, guilt feelings are especially internal and personal, since they result in self-judgement by internalized standards."[12] Guilt often causes people to change their conduct and follow their moral code. Normally guilt feelings can be relieved by confession, an effort to repair any damage that results from the misconduct, a willingness to accept forgiveness, and a determination to look to the future rather than the past. One of the functions of counselors in pastoral ministry is to accept whatever counselees confess and help them derive profit from past mistakes.

Some counselees are never convinced that the slate is clean. Much of the time they feel mildly guilty, sometimes about minor infractions of their ethical and moral code and at other times for no apparent reason at all. They are plagued with a pathological guilt. Severely scrupulous counselees see sin wherever they turn and magnify their transgressions all out of proportion. They experience a free-floating guilt which makes them miserable much of the time. They are overly sensitive to personal responsibilities and obligations. Often they are perfectionists establishing standards of conduct that are totally beyond their reach. Often these guilt-ridden people require the help of a psychiatrist or psychologist.

GRIEF

A final emotion that often comes to the pastoral counselor's attention is grief. In times of sorrow, many people turn to a counselor in pastoral ministry. They find solace in expressing openly their sadness and depression. Grief is a normal reaction to losing someone or something that is highly valued.[13] It is often complicated by other feelings such as hostility, guilt, and depression. The wife whose husband has just died is often plagued by the thought that she was not kind enough during his last illness. Besides experiencing guilt, she also experiences anger toward herself. Most people are able to work through their grief by crying, by talking with other people, or by merely letting time pass. Finding a concerned listener often helps the process. The principal task of the counselor in this case is to create a climate of acceptance and understanding. Counselees who feel that they can talk with someone who cares express their feelings verbally and thus handle them more easily. Frequently this is all they need. With time, the loss is accepted and the individual returns to a state of equilibrium.

Occasionally counselors are asked to talk with people who are unable to overcome their grief. For example, a woman whose husband died a year ago still spends several hours each week at his grave, seldom visits friends and makes no effort to rebuild a new life for herself. She is frequently on the verge of tears and often breaks down when someone mentions her deceased husband. If the usual approaches to pastoral counseling fail, the counselor can be certain that there are deeper pathological causes for her grief and professional care is needed.

OBSTACLES TO UNDERSTANDING

Determining how another person feels is not an easy task. People hide their emotions, especially those that have some social stigma attached; sentimentality is a sign of weakness. We inhibit our emotional reactions and, if questioned about our feelings, deny them or evade the question with a cliché.

 Another obstacle to understanding people's feelings and emotions is that people frequently do not realize how they really feel. From early childhood they learn to repress all undesirable feelings. In adulthood the mechanism works automatically to banish from consciousness many affective reactions. A man who has been passed over for a promotion will probably deny that he feels angry and will say instead that he is just disappointed. He has learned from childhood that it does not pay to express anger openly. After years of repression, he can no longer recognize that he feels frustrated and angry about an injustice. The counselor who wants to convey his understanding to the counselee must somehow surmount these obstacles, indicating that in spite of them he or she has grasped the counselee's real feelings.

CUES TO UNDERSTANDING

Understanding the emotions and feelings of another person demands sensitivity and experience.[14] Counselors should recognize several indicators or cues to a person's feelings. One helpful cue can be taken from an individual's own words. If people are frank, they will tell you what they like and what they dislike. Many people, however, are too fearful to express their feelings verbally. They tell you what they think you want to hear. This is just as likely to occur in pastoral counseling as in a cocktail lounge. People also may indicate their emotions by their manner of speech and gestures. They may not say explicitly that they are angry but show it by their clenched fists and sharp tone of voice. Counselors should be alert to the importance of these signs.

Another cue is the type of emotion associated with a certain situation. When one's car goes into a skid on an icy road, one usually responds with fear or panic. As the counselee describes an argument with his wife, the counselor usually can infer, from his knowledge of how people feel in such a situation, how the counselee feels. From experience most people learn what is the normal affective reaction to a variety of situations. Counselors draw on their experience in attempting to make themselves sensitive to the counselee's feelings.

Finally, counselors use their own affective experience to help them understand the counselee's feelings and emotions. Counselors who have an undistorted awareness of their own reaction to certain situations will be better able to surmise how the counselee feels in a similar situation. Their reactions may differ in some cases, but usually counselors can follow the hypothesis that healthy people have similar emotional experiences.

INTERPLAY OF EMOTIONAL EXPERIENCES

In counseling there is a constant interplay between the emotional experience of the counselee and the counselor. Each is reacting in his or her own way to what is happening in the counseling session. Counselors should be aware of what is taking place both within themselves and within the counselee. A failure to do this can lead to a breakdown in the relationship. Let us consider, for example, the hostile counselee who has conflicting feelings toward authority because of a stern, overly demanding father. This man comes to the pastor's office pouring forth critical, sarcastic remarks about the Church. The pastor's spontaneous reaction is to meet hostility with hostility. Unless the pastor quickly sizes up what is really taking place, he may become involved in a verbal exchange that leads to showing the counselee to the door. In this case the pastor's misunderstanding of the counselee's response leads to a counseling failure. Although the pastor may think that the counselee's feelings are directed at himself or at the Church he represents, actually they spring from the repressive authoritarianism of the counselee's father. They are merely transferred to the pastor, who is identified with his father as an authority figure.[15] Unless the pastor is aware of this transference, he is apt to respond to anger with anger and fail to help the counselee.

Each of us has emotional weak spots, often as a result of the way we were raised. Some feel inadequate in intellectual conversation; others feel rejected by those whom they meet for the first time. Counselors in pastoral ministry usually are no exception; they too have their weak spots. If they are unaware of their weak spots, they may react with hostility toward the counselee who attacks them where they are most vulnerable. Psychiatrists and psychologists frequently undergo psychotherapy to make themselves aware of their weak spots. Counselors in pastoral ministry could benefit from a similar experience since it would afford them the opportunity to come to a greater understanding of their weak spots.

Pastoral counselors should realize that it is normal and healthy for a counselee to express emotions as long as the expression does not harm the counselee or others. There are occasions that call for the expression of anger or fear, even though these occasions may cause discomfort to other people or to counselors themselves. Counselors must express their feelings if they want to be fully human in their dealings with other people. They must learn to accept these emotions for what they are and not resort to repression. They must also learn to accept the counselee's feelings in the same way, even if they are negative and hostile; only by expressing these feelings will the counselee be able to appraise them accurately, evaluate them objectively, and make any necessary changes in his or her attitude.

Feelings and emotions are important motivating forces. The more counselors in pastoral ministry can learn about them and their modes of operation both within themselves and within counselees, the more effective they will be as counselors.

SUMMARY

Even though feelings and emotions are frequently overlooked, feelings and emotions play a dominant role in our psychic lives since they often motivate us to act the way we do. Anxiety, fear, anger, guilt, and grief are the emotional reactions most frequently encountered in counseling. All of these emotions can serve a useful purpose but they can sometimes be painful for the one experiencing them. One of a counselor's primary tasks is to be aware how the counselee feels. Understanding how another feels demands sensitivity and experience. However, there are cues which give some indication of another's feelings.

People handle their emotions in a variety of ways: (1) expressing them openly, (2) channeling them, (3) suppressing them, or (4) repressing them.

In counseling there is a constant interplay between the counselor's and the counselee's emotional experiences. You need to be aware of this interplay and your own feelings and emotions while you are counseling.

5

Coping Strategies

Many who seek pastoral counseling have experienced some kind of breakdown in their coping skills. They find that their usual way of handling a problem is no longer effective. If the situation is important and threatens their sense of well-being and security, anxiety drives them to do something to find a solution. It is usually at this point that they seek out a counselor and hope that the counselor will help them discover ways of coping with their problem.

During our lifetime we each develop a variety of coping skills which allow us to handle almost any situation we encounter. These skills range from the very simple to the complex. Almost from birth infants learn to cope with hunger pangs by crying. They quickly discover that if they cry someone comes and often feeds them. A more complex set of coping skills is exemplified by the young woman who graduates from college as an engineer and takes her first job with an aerospace company. She has had temporary jobs in the aerospace industry before but she has never worked as a part of a team assigned to a special project. Her engineering and mathematical skills learned in college help her to cope with her new position but she must learn new skills if she is to fit in with the team and contribute her share to the special project. Once she has done this, it can be said that she is able to cope with the demands of her new job.

Coping means the adaptive ways we learn to handle conditions of threat, challenge or harm. "In most instances, coping does not demand a single coping act but a wide variety of coping actions, the patterns of which change over time, as the adaptive problem and the psychological state of the individual change."[1] For example, the woman engineer we just mentioned must learn new ways of relating to the men with whom she works and who may harbor some resentment over her entering a field that was once the exclusive domain of men. If there is another woman who is more talented and attractive than she in the department, she will also most probably have to learn how to handle herself and her emotions in dealing with this woman.

There are two types of coping: direct action and palliative coping. In direct action, the individual confronts the situation and takes some appropriate steps to resolve or reduce the threat the situation presents, whereas in palliative coping, the person concentrates on relieving the psychological distress that results from an appraisal of threat or harm.[2]

People whose coping style is mainly taking direct action usually confront a problem and take whatever steps are needed to resolve it. They actively search for information needed to handle the problem and then think it through. They may even anticipate problems before they ever happen and then plan what they intend to do if the situation becomes a problem. If such people seek counseling, they are usually looking for a "sounding board" or someone to confirm the appropriateness of their response to the problem situation.

CHARACTERISTICS OF EFFECTIVE COPING BEHAVIOR

Caplan gives the following characteristics of people whose coping style is effective. (1) They are open to the reality of the situation and seek information which will help them find a solution. (2) They are aware of both their positive and negative feelings and can tolerate frustration. (3) They look for and can accept help from others. (4) Their style of coping includes the ability to break down problems into manageable bits and work through them one at a time. (5) They are flexible and willing to change their view if the situation calls for it. (6) They trust themselves and others and are optimistic about the outcome.[3] People who manifest these characteristics usually seek counseling only if they think they need added information or are looking for a confirming opinion.

Richard Lazarus, an outstanding authority on coping, "suggests that when a threatening event occurs, the individual makes a primary and then a secondary appraisal of the situation. The first appraisal answers the question 'Is there anything at stake here?' This assumes that events can be either (a) irrelevant as far as his or her well-being is concerned (laying off employees at another factory or in another department), (b) benign or positive (receiving a small increase in salary), or (c) stressful. Stressful events in Lazarus's model can be viewed as one of three types. First of all, the event may represent harm or loss (loss of a limb, divorce, untimely death of a loved one). Second, a stressful event may represent a threat to one's present well-being. Third, a stressful event may represent a challenge, an opportunity for growth, mastery or gain. Before coping takes place, the primary appraisal is a cognitive process determining whether or not anything is at stake, and if so, what the stakes are. Secondary appraisal in the Lazarus model is also a cognitive strategy, but it is concerned with coping, that is, 'what to do.' Secondary appraisal aims at changing the situation and managing the subjective components (feelings, thoughts, physical well-being, behavior) related to the situation."[4]

In the model of direct action, individuals have three options: they can attack, withdraw, or compromise.[5] Depending upon the circumstances, each of the three may be appropriate. Let us consider the dismissal of an employee under circumstances which she considers unjust. If she uses the method of attack, she takes her case to a union grievance committee and seeks to be reinstated. If she opts for withdrawal, she simply leaves the job and seeks other employment. In the case of withdrawal, the woman admits defeat, gives up, and tries to find a new job. If she seeks a compromise, she approaches her supervisor and tries to be transferred to another department of the same company or a satellite company. In this case, the person realizes that she cannot achieve her desired goal and settles for a substitute. Which approach is appropriate will depend upon the environmental situation and her emotional state. Sometimes the task of the counselor is to help the individual see what her options are and then decide upon the one which best fits her situation.

Coping can also be palliative, which means that the individual tries to handle the distressing situation by means other than direct action. In this case the emphasis is on relieving the emotional distress caused by the anxiety-provoking situation. Using defense mechanisms is an example of palliative coping.

DEFENSE MECHANISMS

The human mind has many ways of escaping the intolerable. One of Sigmund Freud's major contributions to understanding human behavior is his treatise on defense mechanisms.[6] Somewhat later Miller and Dollard subjected this theory to more rigorous research and placed it on a more scientific foundation.[7] When we are unable to face threatening stresses we sometimes resort to defense tactics. The particular tactic that we use is the product of experience and learning. Frequent repetition makes it an habitual response, part of our usual repertoire of responses. Each time we use a defense mechanism, we lessen our anxiety—and as a result we come to rely more and more on that particular defense mechanism.

As small children we learn that a direct confrontation with parental authority leads to frustration, anxiety, guilt, and possibly punishment; yet we still want our own way. We learn devious ways of coping with this disturbing situation. Frequently our coping techniques are quite similar to those used by our parents. The girl who hears her mother wiggle out of a detested parent-teacher committee meeting on the grounds of a terrible headache may soon use the same excuse when faced with a test at school. And strangely enough the daughter actually has a headache. Repetition makes the excuse as routine as tying one's shoes. Although each time that people use a defense mechanism they lessen anxiety and tension, no defense is fully effective.[8] In most instances part of the anxiety lingers in the back of the mind. Sometimes the defense brings on new stress, even though it lessens anxiety. The girl who develops headaches to avoid taking examinations soon discovers that she is failing in school, and she is subjected to new pressures both at school and at home. Some defenses, as we shall see, interfere with effective functioning. A further limitation of defensive coping devices is the exorbitant amount of energy they require. Even though we are not aware of the price we are paying to lessen anxiety and fear, the maintenance of an extensive defense system saps much of the energy that could be used in more constructive pursuits.

NEED FOR DEFENSE MECHANISMS

The above discussion should not lead to the conclusion that all defense mechanisms are harmful.[9] Some are very necessary for psychological equilibrium. Were we suddenly to be stripped of our defenses, we could have a mental breakdown. This is especially true in the case of the person with a weak ego and limited mental health. At times it is healthy to sidestep an issue for a while; to meet it head-on would only bring disaster. In such instances our use of defense mechanisms may protect us from damage to our personality.

In attempting to understand someone who comes for help, counselors in pastoral ministry should attempt to recognize the unique characteristics of the counselee's defense system. Such recognition is necessary not to persuade the person to abandon debilitating defenses, but rather to communicate an understanding of the counselee's world. This communicated understanding may cause the counselee to see that he or she is making use of a particular defense mechanism and sometimes recognize the reason for using the defense. The purpose of pastoral counseling, however, is not to bring about a change in the counselee's defense structure, which sometimes is a goal in psychotherapy, but rather to help the counselee make use of his or her existing personality strengths in solving a problem in accordance with the principles of Christian living.

DENIAL AND REPRESSION

Denial is an example of a basic defense mechanism. By denying that a problem exists, people avoid the anxiety that the problem might provoke and the need to confront it.[10] A somewhat similar device is repression.[11] In this defense individuals unconsciously block from their awareness certain feelings and impulses. For example, a wife may be very angry about her husband's belittling attitude, but she experiences only a feeling of indifference. By constantly telling herself that his attitude really does not make any difference, she reaches the state where she is no longer aware of her anger. Although repression is one of our most frequently used defenses, we seldom realize when we are using this defense.

MORE EXAMPLES OF DEFENSE REACTIONS

During the course of a working day, the counselor in pastoral ministry meets many types of defense mechanisms. Let us consider some examples.

A father whose teenage son has become involved with the juvenile authorities because of drug abuse and theft comes to a counselor for help. He is obviously shaken by the incident. At one point in the discussion, he makes this statement: "I have been so busy with my work that I really have not given the boy the time I should have." If the father had better self-understanding, he would have had to admit that he was using a defense tactic to avoid facing the fact that he is failing as a parent. The tactic that he is using is called rationalization. We do not like to admit failure in one of life's main obligations and so we devise a way of excusing ourselves.

Another common defense is projection.[12] A forty year old, overly pious, unmarried woman comes to discuss her deteriorating personal relationships. She is convinced that most of the women in the office where she works are talking about her behind her back. She thinks that they are jealous over special favors she has received from her employer. As the interview progresses, it becomes clear that the woman has only vague and inconsistent evidence for her convictions. She is physically unattractive and has a bland personality. In many respects she has rejected herself and resorts to projection to avoid admitting this to herself. She blocks the reality of her self-hatred from consciousness and instead attributes this feeling of hatred to other people. To justify her position she imagines that her fellow workers are jealous over special favors she has received from her employer. This psychological device allows her to divert her attention away from her poor opinion of herself.

One type of repression is called emotional insulation.[13] A haggard-looking mother of four small children comes for help in dealing with an alcoholic husband. She is vivacious and dynamic. After a few pleasantries, she launches into the heart-rending description of her life with an alcoholic husband and his inability to support his family. At the conclusion of a depressing account of poverty and struggle, she remarks, "My husband's drinking really does not bother me. I am just concerned about his spiritual welfare because I love him so much." She has found that the only way she can live is by refusing to allow her true feelings to come into consciousness. She denies that she feels concern or anxiety. She has a sick child and no medication. There is little food in the house, but somehow she says God will provide. She speaks of God's love for her and her family. She gives no indication of being angry at her husband or her situation. She does not permit her fears about the future or anxiety over her sick child to surface. As a consequence, she does not face her problem and take steps to improve the situation. Within the same parish she may have a counterpart who has solved her inner problems by dedicating herself to personal "holiness." This woman attends every event that happens at her church. You will find her at prayer meetings, novenas, daily Mass and often at more than one Mass on Sundays. The purpose of all this activity is to divert attention from her real problem, such as loneliness or feelings of rejection. As long as most of her life is taken up with religious functions, there is no time to worry about anything else. Furthermore being "holy" does enhance her view of herself. Of course, not everyone who goes to prayer meetings and various church ceremonies is motivated by unconscious defense mechanisms.

A final example is the man who, because of his defense tactics, never comes to the counselor's office at all. He uses isolation as a means of self-protection.[14] He finds withdrawing from reality a most convenient coping device. He finds that he can no longer battle the world, so he retreats to the safety of his home and rarely ventures out. He engages in endless daydreaming, hours of TV and reading novels. Rather than face failure, he builds a more tolerable world within his imagination. It is usually a distraught parent or relative who approaches the counselor in pastoral ministry and seeks advice about helping such an individual.

COPING STYLES

Each of us has his or her own style of coping. No two are exactly alike. Most of us combine the direct action approach with a variety of defense mechanisms. Which of the two predominates depends upon the situation. In attempting to help counselees, you need to size up the person's strengths and weaknesses in coping strategies. One of the ways of doing this is to ask the person if he or she has ever faced the same or a similar problem before, and then you ask what he or she did about it. If the counselee indicates that he or she confronted the problem and took definite steps to resolve it, you then have some evidence of the counselee's ability to take direct action when confronted with a problem. If the person goes on to tell you that this is his or her usual way of handling problems, you have a further confirmation of the person's coping strengths.

If, on the other hand, the counselee tells you that he or she did nothing about the problem but simply waited it out, saying that time heals everything, you have evidence of evasive tactics in handling problems. When such people face a problem, they usually cope by inaction and deny that the problem is really a situation that disrupts their lives.

WHY INQUIRE ABOUT COPING SKILLS?

People who seek pastoral counseling usually come with a problem. Your task as a counselor is to help the person find a solution to the problem that he or she thinks can be put into action. If the individual has strong coping skills, then your task is simply to give some structure to the process (we shall address the process of problem-solving in a later chapter) and act as a sounding board. If, on the other hand, the counselee is extremely defensive, then your task is going to be much more difficult, and it may even be that there is no solution, at least for the time being, in which case the most you have to offer the counselee is the support that comes from being an interested and understanding listener. Your proposing a solution is too threatening and, although he or she may express appreciation for the help you have given, the odds of the counselee's using your solution are minimal. Getting some indication of the counselee's coping tactics can keep you from making a counseling error and save you a lot of time.

REDUCING DEFENSIVENESS

One of the first tasks in any form of counseling is to create an atmosphere that lessens the counselee's feeling of anxiousness. As long as counselees feel anxious and uneasy, they remain defensive and probably will be unable to look at their problem in its true perspective.

You should try to make your counselees feel more secure and be more open to reality. The more facts that counselees can perceive and evaluate, the better are their chances of finding a solution to their problem. If their views are distorted or limited to a small, disturbing aspect of the situation, they will overlook many circumstances that are important for a correct evaluation. One common distortion is to magnify possible consequences of the difficulty beyond reasonable proportions. In this case, the person needs the opportunity to talk freely and openly without fear of being judged or deprecated for having a problem. The counselor must be careful lest his or her attitude causes the counselee to feel threatened.

Counseling can be a threatening experience. A counselor in pastoral ministry, like any other counselor, must make every effort to lessen the element of threat and help the counselees face the reality of their situation. Effective counseling begins when counselees can say "I do know" or "I can face it" or "It is I" (and not someone else).[15] In some ways pastoral counselors have a more difficult assignment than psychological counselors. Their role as clergy or dedicated persons set them on a pedestal; they are looked upon as exemplary people with high ideals and values. Often counselees feel that they cannot live up to the expectations of these special people. You as a pastoral counselor should try to do everything possible to offset this attitude of counselees and create a non-threatening attitude. There are certain procedures that can be avoided and others that can be used. Perhaps the most important thing to avoid is any mannerism or expression that would indicate an attitude of superiority. If you give the impression that you have all the answers because of your superior education, you immediately belittle your counselees and make them feel inferior, with the result that they strengthen their defenses to protect what self-esteem they have left.

JUDGMENT AND DEFENSE REACTIONS

From early childhood people have passed judgments on our actions. Negative judgments often put us on the defensive.[16] When eight year old Johnny tears the knee of his pants while skating, his mother greets him with "You are a bad boy; you tore your pants." Johnny immediately replies, "I didn't do it. Jimmy pushed me." Mother has made a negative judgment which weakened Johnny's self-esteem and Johnny reacted by becoming defensive. Many adults have not changed their defensive reactions essentially from the time when they were children except for finding more complex ways of defending themselves. If counselors assume the role of parents and pass judgment on the actions of counselees, they are likely to hear the same response that Johnny's mother heard, only stated in a more sophisticated way. Judgmental statements should have limited use in pastoral counseling. Circumstances may occasionally arise which call for such statements, since many pastoral counselors are also teachers of Christian morality and will sometimes be asked whether a particular action is right or wrong; but they should use this procedure sparingly.

Most people who have relatively stable personalities either understand the moral implications of their actions already or, if given some basic principles, can easily draw their own conclusions. They do not need someone to tell them that they are doing wrong. Dwelling on the sinfulness of their actions can only increase defensiveness and feelings of guilt.

It hardly seems necessary to point out that there is seldom, if ever, an occasion for "hell and damnation" exhortations in pastoral counseling. Such an approach increases feelings of fear and anxiety and makes it more difficult for counselees to face objectively the problems that beset them.

SUMMARY

Many who seek counseling have had some kind of a breakdown in their coping skills. By coping is meant the typical way or ways we have learned to handle a particular situation. When one of these ways of coping ceases to be effective, we experience increased anxiety which motivates us to look for other ways of handling the situation. It is at this time that people often seek the help of a counselor in pastoral ministry.

Defense mechanisms, such as repression, rationalization and projection, make up a part of our coping strategy. While the use of some defensive tactics is expected and necessary, an overuse of these tactics is frequently characteristic of a neurotic disorder. Counselors in pastoral ministry need to be aware of the counselee's defense mechanisms not to change them but so as to have a better understanding of what the counselee is experiencing and be in a better position to help these counselees.

6

Listening and Responding
to the Message

In each counseling session there is usually a message that the counselee wants to give the counselor. The message is often the thing that prompted the person to seek help. The message can be anything from "My wife and I are not getting along; we are constantly arguing and fighting," to "Life is the pits; I'm all mixed up and don't know what to do." It may be clearly expressed or it may be garbled and confused. The message is what the counselee wants the counselor to hear and respond to. The primary task of the counselor is to unwrap the message.

The message usually has: (1) content, (2) an emotional or feeling component, and (3) meaning. All three are important and need to be considered if the counseling is going to help the counselee.

CONTENT OF THE MESSAGE

The content is the matter being discussed. It is usually a description of events that are or have taken place in the person's life. More often than not, the content involves other people and the way the counselee is reacting to these other people. Effective counselors try to understand as fully as possible what is going on in the person's life, and then give some indication that they do understand, even if it is only by a nod of the head or an "umhum."

Let us consider the following case and note the content of the person's message. A mother of three teenagers comes to the parish office and seeks help. While she was doing the family laundry, she discovered marijuana in the pants pocket of her youngest son. She was shocked and angry and blamed herself. She says she did not have this kind of trouble with the two older children and could not understand why the youngest would do such a thing. At considerable sacrifice, she had sent all three children to parochial schools because she heard that public schools had drug problems. She expressed disappointment in the parochial school system. She told how the youngest son had always been more independent and more subject to peer pressure than the other two. Also, she noted that whenever he seemed to be troubled, he never sought advice from either his father or herself. She blamed herself for not giving him more attention and not monitoring more closely the friends with whom he associated. She said she did not know what to do and was seeking advice.

In this example the message is "I discovered that my youngest son is using marijuana and I don't know what to do about it." There are also a number of details that add to the basic meaning of the message, such as the age of her son, his friends, her attitude toward the use of marijuana, the son's openness to peer pressure, the school he attends, etc. You as counselor need to indicate in some way that you have heard the message and all the details of the message. If you simply listen and never give any indication that you have heard what was said, the counselee never knows whether you have really heard and understood what was said. There are a couple of skills that you can use to let the counselee know that you understand the message—or at least are trying to understand it. One of these is to restate what was said; another is to summarize the essential elements of what was said. Restating what was said is sometimes called paraphrasing.[1] We paraphrase when we take what the person has said and put it in our own words. It is different from parroting which restates what the person has said in approximately the same words that the person used. Paraphrasing indicates to the counselee that you have heard what was said and understand it, at least enough to be able to put it in your own words. Since you have phrased the counselee's statement in somewhat different words, the counselee may also get a different perspective on what he or she has said. Other dividends of paraphrasing are: (1) it helps the counselor remember what was said; (2) it stops escalating anger and helps to cool down the counselee; (3) it keeps the counselor from yielding to the temptation to judge and give advice.

Another skill you can use is summarizing, which usually takes place after counselees have described the essential elements of what they see as the problem.[2] After listening to the story of the person who has come to you for help, you might make a statement such as "Let me see if I have understood you correctly. You say that you . . ." and then you describe the essential elements of the problem as you have heard them. Summarizing ties the parts of the message together and allows the counselee to see the whole picture. It may also prompt the counselee to correct any misunderstanding on your part or add what seems to have been overlooked. Not infrequently, the summary causes the counselee to give a fuller description of his or her situation.

If you do not understand what the counselee has said, it helps neither you nor the counselee to pretend you understand by nodding your head or saying "I understand." Eventually it will become apparent to the counselee that you do not understand, and then the counselee's trust in you as a counselor is diminished. If you do not understand what the counselee is saying, it is best to indicate that you do not understand and then ask the person to clarify what he or she has just said. Using a couple of well formulated questions usually clears up the matter.[3]

FEELINGS AND EMOTIONS

In addition to content, most messages indicate how counselees feel about what they have said. These feelings are often as important, if not more important, than the content of the message. In their desire to bring the counselee to a quick solution, some counselors overlook how the counselee feels about the content of the message. This is a mistake because much of our motivation comes not from how we think but how we feel.[4] Usually counselees have some definite feelings about the problem they present. It may make them happy or sad, angry or fearful. Sometimes counselees are aware of how they feel; at other times, they are not. In either case, it is helpful to let counselees know how they feel. In the former instance, reflecting how they feel underscores the feelings or emotions for them; in the latter, reflecting brings to their awareness how they feel. This process of letting people know that you understand how they feel is called empathetic understanding.[5] Empathetic understanding involves two elements: (1) being aware of how the person feels, and (2) communicating to this person that you understand how he or she feels.

Carl Rogers describes empathetic understanding as follows: "It means entering the private perceptual world of the other and becoming thoroughly at home in it. It involves being sensitive, moment by moment, to the changing meanings which flow in this other person, to the fear or rage or tenderness or confusion or whatever he or she is experiencing. It means temporarily living in the other's life, moving about in it delicately without making judgments; it means sensing meanings of which he or she is scarcely aware, but not trying to uncover totally unconscious feelings, since this would be too threatening. It includes communicating your sensings of the person's world as you look with fresh and unfrightening eyes at elements of which he or she is fearful. It means frequently checking with the person as to the accuracy of your sensings, and being guided by the response you receive."[6]

Let us consider once again the example of the woman who found marijuana in her son's pants pocket. This woman's emotional response when she discovered that her son was smoking marijuana is shock and anger. She also implies that she feels guilty because she thinks she has failed as a parent. She expresses disappointment and perhaps some anger at the parochial school system. It is helpful for this woman to realize how she feels and to know that another understands how she feels and does not judge her for having these feelings. It is also helpful for her to recognize the emotions that she may not fully realize she had, such as her guilt because she sees herself as an inadequate parent and her disappointment with the Catholic school system. Part of helping this woman is to allow her to air how she feels and then to assist her to come to terms with these emotions.

ACKNOWLEDGING FEELINGS AND EMOTIONS

Acknowledging the feeling component usually calls for some kind of a response which reflects how the person feels. For example the counselor might say to this woman: "Finding marijuana in your son's pocket must have been a real shock to you. Now you seem to be angry at him and yourself and don't know what to do." This response centers the woman's attention on how she felt when she discovered the marijuana, how she presently feels, and it lets her know that another understands what she has experienced and is presently experiencing within herself. More important, it lets her see that another accepts her and how she feels without passing judgment on either her or her son. It offers no advice; it puts no pressure on her to take any action. It frees her to make the decision she thinks best, and yet offers to be with her as she tries to decide what to do and then to help her act on the decision she makes.

WHAT IS THE VALUE OF EMPATHETIC UNDERSTANDING?

First of all, it makes people feel that they have a partner in facing a distressing situation.[7] She is not alone. There is someone else who understands her dilemma and how she feels about it. This understanding gives the counselee a sense of inner security and places her in a position to make a decision and act on it. Secondly, it makes this woman feel valued, cared for, and accepted for the person that she is. And, finally, it helps her come to a fuller understanding of herself and her situation. Usually empathetic responses cause people to talk more freely and openly about themselves and their problem. As a consequence, they come to understand what is taking place within themselves and then they are in a better position to cope with their problem.

MEANING

Meaning is the third dimension of the message. Words are symbols that represent a reality. Each word we use has a meaning that is common for all who use the word, and yet at the same time each word has a meaning that is unique for each of us. For example, the word "home" is a symbol for a dwelling place where a group of people live together in unity. The word has a common meaning that is understood by all and then it has a meaning that is unique. The high school senior who was raised in the armed services and has moved twelve times since he was born has a very different understanding of the word "home" than the young man who has lived all his life in the same house, in a large, closely-knit family, and in a small rural community. Past experiences give a unique meaning to our understanding of words. It is the task of the counselor to get inside the mind of the counselee and try to understand these unique meanings.

Understanding what the counselee means also means understanding how the counselee looks at the world.[8] We sometimes tend to think that others look at the world in the same way we do. Good counselors are quick to enter into the counselee's world of meanings. They can put aside their own point of view for the moment and see what the counselee understands by what he or she is saying, and then indicate this by paraphrasing or reflecting.

Understanding the meaning counselees give to what they say is especially important for counselors in pastoral ministry because faith often determines how counselees look at the particular situation they are facing. The committed Christian looks at the gradual disintegration of a marriage in a way quite different from the non-believer. Most Catholics know that divorce and remarriage excludes them from the sacramental life of the Church, and this belief usually plays a significant role in the final decision as to what they should do, which may not be an issue for those who are not committed to any religious belief.

LISTENING TO THE MESSAGE

Listening is the most important of all the skills used in counseling. Without attentive listening there can be no understanding of the counselee's message.[9] Most of us assume that we listen when someone speaks to us, so we usually do not see it as a counseling skill. We do not think that we need to learn how to listen. It just comes naturally. However, when educators in counseling speak of listening, they have in mind something quite different from the listening one does in a conversation. When we as counselors listen, we give our total and undivided attention not only to what is being said but to how it is being said. We even go so far as to note what is not said. We do not focus on what we are going to say next, as frequently happens in conversation. For the time being, we suspend all categorizing and diagnosing. We pass no judgments. We simply listen to what the counselee is saying and then we ask ourselves what this person is experiencing right now and/ or what this person has experienced in the past. We then try to imagine how we would feel if we were in this person's shoes. This kind of listening demands a conscious effort on our part to listen to everything the person has to say without approving or disapproving what is said.

We listen not only with our minds, hearts, and imagination but with our whole person.[10] Along with hearing the actual words of the counselee, we pay attention to non-verbal cues, such as tone of voice, facial expression, gestures, body posture and mode of dress. For example, an elderly man may respond to your question "How are things going?" with "Just fine," but the tone of his voice and an expression of sadness in his face tells you there is an incongruence between the spoken message and the true message. If the counselor listens just to the person's words, the true message can be missed.

VERBAL, PARAVERBAL, AND NON-VERBAL

The counselee's message usually involves three components: (1) the verbal, (2) the paraverbal, and (3) the non-verbal. The verbal consists of the words used to express thoughts, feelings and meanings. The paraverbal is the way the information is given and includes such elements as tone of voice, pace and manner of speech.[11] For example, depressed people tend to speak more slowly and in a lower tone than usual. If they are severely depressed, their sentence structure may be disjointed. On the other hand, the anxious person will usually speak more rapidly and in a higher pitch.

In expressing the message, counselees often make use of body language. One of the best indicators of how people feel is their facial expression. When we are happy our eyes light up and we smile; when we feel apathetic, our eyes are listless and we generally frown. Happiness, anger, fear, surprise and sadness, all have typical facial expressions. From early childhood we learn to react to people's body language. We usually pick up how others feel from the expression on their faces. If you say something the counselee does not like, you can usually surmise this from the expression on the counselee's face. It is also helpful to realize that your facial expression tells the counselee how you are reacting to what the counselee has just said.

When we are interested in what people are saying, we tend to lean forward and fix our gaze on the other person's eyes; when we are disinterested, we tend to slouch in the chair and occasionally glance off into space. Our body language tells the counselee whether we are interested or bored.

Clothes and personal hygiene offer further clues to the meaning of the counselee's message. People who deviate radically from their usual mode of dress and hygienic care of themselves may be trying to tell you something. Depressed people usually lose interest in their personal appearance. A depressed woman sometimes may look disheveled—her dress is wrinkled with a couple of buttons missing, her hair is uncombed, and she uses no make-up. The message she is trying to give is: "I don't like myself; I have lost all respect for myself." The older man who dresses like college students and imitates their hair style may be saying: "I consider myself a young man; I'm not middle-aged." These few examples should highlight the importance of non-verbal cues in trying to listen to the true message. Non-verbal listening demands concentration and the constant use of one's perceptive powers. It is a skill that does not come naturally but can be learned with effort and practice.

Sometimes what people don't say is more important than what they do say. For instance, an obviously overweight young high school teacher who is afraid that her teaching contract will not be renewed next year comes to you for counseling. She mentions several problems she has had while teaching during the past year but never her weight problem and her failure to do anything about it, even though her principal has made reference to her being overweight and the impact this might have on her teenage students with a similar problem.

THE VALUE OF LISTENING

Why is listening an essential ingredient of effective counseling? First of all, it is needed if the counselor is to understand what the counselee is consciously or unconsciously trying to say. Without it the counselor can miss an important part of the message. Moreover, active listening shows people that you are interested in them as individuals. It tells people that you respect and are concerned about them.

Active listening also causes people to ventilate their feelings. When people feel understood, they are much more likely to speak about how they feel. As people speak about how they feel, they get their feelings and emotions out in the open, come to understand them better, and then are in a position to handle them better. And, finally, the counselor's listening causes the counselee to focus more sharply on the topic they want to discuss rather than talk around it.

OBSTACLES

What are some obstacles that hinder effective listening? Probably the greatest obstacle is centering one's attention on the problem and its solution rather than on the subjective experience of the counselee. Some counselors have "canned" solutions to a number of typical problems. They listen for indications of a particular problem and then give the same advice that they had previously used.

As a consequence, these counselors sometimes fail to hear the real problem but concentrate their attention on what they think is the problem. Had they centered their attention on what the counselee was saying and feeling, the real problem would have emerged and they would then have been in a position to help the person find a solution to the problem.

Another obstacle to listening is selective listening. In selective listening, the counselor listens to what he or she wants to hear. For example, a woman counselor who is trying to help another woman with a marriage problem unconsciously sides with the woman's grievances against her husband and fails to hear the woman's subtle indications that she may be equally at fault in the breakdown of the marriage.

Still another is a personal conflict that the counselor has and has never fully worked through, such as the physical and psychological pain the counselor experienced at the hands of a brutal, alcoholic father.[12] When the counselee speaks about something that calls to mind this painful experience, the counselor no longer is able to attend to what the counselee is saying because his or her mind is caught up in past memories and feelings.

And, finally, distractions can become obstacles to listening. These distractions can be either interior or exterior. Unless we make a concerted effort, our minds tend to wander. This is especially true of people who have other responsibilities and tend to worry about these responsibilities. When our minds are on other matters, we lose a whole section of the counselee's message—and that section could be the most important. Distractions can also be exterior or coming from something outside of us, such as the ringing of a telephone or someone talking outside the window. Inasmuch as possible, counseling should be carried on in an environment that is relatively free from exterior distractions. When this is not possible, it is good to let the counselee know that you are trying to listen but that you are being distracted.

GETTING AT THE CORE OF THE MESSAGE

The central topic which the person wishes to discuss is called the core of the message.[13] The core usually has content, feeling and meaning. It is your task as counselor to focus your attention on the core of the message and then reflect this core to the counselee so that the counselee will see that you understand it. You are then in a position to help the counselee find a way to solve the problem.

The core message of some people is easily understood. With little or no encouragement, these people describe their situation in a methodical, well organized manner. All you need to do is listen and occasionally reflect what they have said so as to indicate you are with them and understand what they are saying. Then when you have heard their whole story, you should give what you think is the heart of the problem they have presented.

Some people, however, are confused and the core of their message is lost in a jungle of details and tangents that seem to be going nowhere. In this case, your task as counselor is to dig out the core of the message and then reflect it back to the counselee to check and see if it is accurate. When you present the core of the message, the counselee may respond by saying: "Yes, what you say is right," or she may want to qualify what you have said with "Yes, that is right but I don't think I am resentful over what he did," or she may simply deny it by saying: "No, it is not that way at all." The counselee's last two statements allow you to correct what you have said and bring your response more in line with the counselee's thinking and feeling. Once both you and the counselee have a clear picture of what is happening in the counselee's life, then the counseling process is ready to move forward.

Sometimes the counselee's expressed message is incomplete or not clear. One of the ways to clarify what the counselee is trying to say is to use a question. There are two kinds of questions: open-ended and closed.[14] Open-ended questions are those that cannot be answered with a simple "Yes" or "No" or one or two words. They give the person the opportunity to respond in a number of different ways. An example is "How did you feel about that?" or "What are your thoughts about leaving him?" The function of the open-ended question is to get the person to open up and talk more about a topic. It is a way of keeping the dialogue going but at the same time it frequently adds more data and information about the core message. The second type of question is the closed question. The closed question asks for a specific response and does not allow the counselee to develop any topic he or she may want to develop. Examples of a closed question are "How many children do you have?" or "Where do you live now?"

Usually in the beginning of the dialogue we use open-ended questions because we want the person to talk about what is important to him or her. Frequently counselors find that they can get most of the information they need to help the person by asking open-ended questions. If you encourage counselees to talk, they will usually give a fairly complete and accurate picture of their situation. If, after the person has given his or her story, you need more information to get a clearer picture, you can then ask some closed questions. If you are not sure what the counselee meant by a statement, you can use a closed question to clarify the meaning. An example of this might be: "I am wondering if the decision you made is definite; you seem to be expressing some hesitation. Am I hearing you correctly?" This procedure clears up the ambiguous and gives the counselee the opportunity to develop further the topic under discussion. It also allows you to check on the accuracy of what you think you have heard.

GUIDELINES FOR ASKING QUESTIONS

Here are some guidelines for asking questions:

1. Ask one question at a time. When you bombard people with several questions, they are unable to remember all of them and usually answer only one. By the time they have answered the one, they have forgotten the others.
2. Keep your questions short and to the point. Long, vague questions tend to confuse people.
3. In formulating the question, be sure to take into consideration the person's education; use words he or she can understand.
4. Avoid asking a "why" question, such as "Why did you do that?" People can take a "why" question as a reprehension

and get defensive. Ask "How," "Where" and "What" questions.

5. Avoid using questions to give advice, such as "Don't you think you ought to call your mother?" If you think you need to offer advice, give it directly.

6. Be careful about asking leading questions. The skillful use of a series of questions can lead counselees to your conclusions, often without their really accepting these conclusions. Leading questions can be a way of imposing your solution to a problem on the counselee.

FOCUSING THE DIALOGUE

So as to get the person to look at every feature of what is happening, it may be necessary at times to change the focus of the dialogue.[15] The focus can be on the persons themselves, on others, such as a spouse or friend, on the situation, such as a job or family; it can be on the past, present or future. Once counselees have fully discussed one aspect of a problem, a nudge may be needed to get them to turn their attention to another aspect. The process whereby this is achieved is called changing the focus. For example, a woman with a marriage problem may have thoroughly developed how she and her husband relate to one another but then seems unable to get off the topic. You may have to question her about her relationship with her children.

Some people tend to drift from one topic to another without ever fully developing any one of them. Others talk around a subject without ever getting to the heart of the matter. These people need assistance to help them focus on one topic and then keep them on this topic. This can be done by bringing to their attention a matter they had just mentioned and you feel is important. You could say: "A few minutes ago you spoke about your friend. Could you tell me a little more about this friend?"

Some have a tendency to avoid talking about themselves. They want you to tell them how they can change other people, not themselves. A husband may be willing to talk about his wife's problem but not his own. If you fall into the trap and allow the dialogue to focus on possible ways of changing the behavior of the wife, you free this man from the responsibility of looking at himself and probably undermine the beneficial effects the counseling might have on him. This man needs to be encouraged in a tactful manner to look at himself and what he might be doing to cause his wife to act in the way she does. Your discussing with counselees the problem of another can lead these counselees to believe that the other person has a problem and they do not.

A common error in counseling is to shift the focus inadvertently before the topic has been fully discussed. For instance, when the discussion is on a wife's relationship with her husband, the counselor interjects: "And how are your children reacting to your fighting?" Immediately the counselee's attention is diverted to her children and may never return to the relationship issue, which has not yet been fully discussed.

SUMMARY

In a dialogue there is a message the speaker wishes to convey to the counselor. This message has content, feeling and meaning. The counselor's main task is to focus his or her whole attention on this message and try to understand the core of this message. The counselor then needs to communicate to the counselee that the intended message is understood.

The message may be found not only in what people say,

but also in the way they say it, their body language and personal appearance, and even what they do not say.

There are a number of counseling skills which help the counselor communicate to the counselee that he or she understands the full message, such as active listening, reflecting content and feeling, summarizing, clarifying, questioning and focusing. Learning to use these attending and listening skills can greatly improve the effectiveness of your counseling.

7

Influencing the Counselee

Attending, listening and reflecting skills focus on the person's inner world. The aim of these skills is to get people to come to a fuller understanding of themselves and their situation, and thus be in a position to make any changes in themselves or their environment that may be needed. Effective attending and listening occurs when the counselor tries to understand the counselee's message from the counselee's point of view. There are times when the use of listening and reflecting skills is sufficient to help counselees resolve whatever brings them to counseling, but there are also times when you need to move beyond listening and reflecting and make use of influencing skills.

Counseling can be described as a process of interpersonal influence.[1] Attending and listening affect counselees indirectly whereas influencing skills affect them directly. The effective use of influencing skills stems from the counselor's empathetic understanding of the counselee's situation from the counselee's frame of reference. When counselors fail to understand what the counselee is going through from the counselee's point of view, they run the risk of using influencing skills incorrectly or trying to help counselees solve a problem that actually is not the counselee's problem but what the counselor thinks is his or her problem.

The influencing skills most frequently used in pastoral counseling are: (1) Giving information, (2) Instructing, (3) Reassuring, (4) Confronting, (5) Leading, and (6) Suggesting and Giving Advice. The aim of these skills is to help people change their ways of thinking, feeling, acting and relating to others, and thus become better able to handle the problem that brings them to counseling.

GIVING INFORMATION

Giving information is supplying a person with facts and data about experiences, events, and people; frequently, these facts and data give the person another way of looking at a situation and then may offer other possible solutions to a problem.[2] There are times when all the counselee needs is information. Take for example the woman who is in marriage counseling and comes to seek information about an annulment. Assuming that the marriage counseling has been effective, this woman needs to learn whether she is eligible for an annulment and what are her chances of getting an annulment. To withhold this information because you think this woman has a personal problem that needs to be handled does this woman a disservice because it deprives her of the opportunity to consider a possible alternative in her search for a solution to her marriage problem.

When should information be given? The most obvious answer is when the person asks for information. Usually the counselor who listens attentively knows when the counselees are seeking information, when they are testing the counselor to see how he or she will respond, or when they are asking for information as a means of leading into what they really want to talk about. When people indicate dissatisfaction with your answer, it may be that they are not seeking information but just testing to see what stance you are going to take. Once you have committed yourself, they will then reveal the real reason for their coming or terminate the dialogue as quickly as they can. Others may ask an information-seeking question to test whether you are going to pass judgment on their behavior or not.

Sometimes counselors give information without the counselee ever asking for it because they think the information might help the counselee at a later time. Usually offering information that has little or no reference to the matter being discussed has minimal influence on people. They either do not hear it or they quickly forget it.

Without their realizing it, some counselees need to know about certain facts if they are going to resolve a problem. An example is the teenager who has become pregnant and needs to know that there are other options besides getting an abortion. It is up to the counselor to inform her of the other possible options. Or again, counselees sometimes have incorrect beliefs that need correcting, like the woman who thinks that separation from a husband who physically abuses her is morally wrong.

Sometimes people are unable to see the consequences of their decisions, such as the woman separated from her husband who loves her independence but decides to fight a court battle for full custody of her two small children without taking into consideration that she will be tied down caring for these children without any assistance from her former husband. Such a person needs someone to point out to her the consequences of her decision, lest these consequences cause her and her children unhappiness.

Information should be given in a matter of fact manner. It should not be imposed but simply stated. An authoritative, know-it-all attitude can be annoying and cause the counselee to disregard the information.

GUIDELINES FOR GIVING INFORMATION

Here are some guidelines for giving information.

1. Be sure that the information you give is correct. If you are not sure or do not know the information, look it up and have the person return.
2. Do not give information as factual that is simply your opinion.
3. Information should be worded in such a way that it is easily understood. Many people do not understand theological language.
4. Timing is important. Information should be given when the counselee needs information and is ready to accept it, which means that you may have to prepare the ground before you give the information.
5. Be aware that some information can have an emotional impact on a person. After giving the information, you need to discuss with the person the impact that the information is having.
6. Overloading the counselee with too much information can be confusing. Give information in small doses.
7. Do not shy away from giving unpleasant information simply because you find it too hard to give this information.[3]

INSTRUCTING

Giving instruction is another influencing skill. Instruction means showing people what they should do, how they should act, or what they should avoid.[4] People sometimes need to be taught how they should act, especially when they find themselves in a new situation. Take for example the mother of the teenaged son who is smoking marijuana, given in the previous chapter. Since this is her first encounter with this problem the counselor may decide to tell her how she should act rather than merely assist her to come to a decision as to what she should do. The counselor might say something like this to her, "I think that it would help you to follow this course of action: tell your son that you found marijuana in his pocket and that you are worried about him and his health. Perhaps later on you could tell him a bit about the adverse effects of using marijuana. As far as we know the effects of continuous use of marijuana are these . . ." Instruction differs from advice inasmuch as the one giving the instruction teaches the person something he or she did not know whereas in giving advice the counselor suggests or advises a certain course of action, which usually the person has already considered.

Instruction calls for a direct approach. When a person needs to learn about another way of solving a problem, or must act and has little or no experience to fall back on, or is so emotionally distressed that he or she is unable to make a decision, then instruction has a valid place in counseling.

GUIDELINES ON INSTRUCTION

Here are some guidelines on giving instruction.

1. Fit the instruction to the person. Give the instruction in language that the person can easily understand. Make it simple.
2. Once you have given the instruction, check to see if the

person understands it. Often it helps to get the person to summarize what you have said.

3. Try not to be dogmatic. It is best to avoid such statements as, "You should do this." Rather say, "I think it would help you to take the following steps."

4. Point out reasons for following the instructions.[5]

REASSURANCE

For a variety of reasons some people feel that they are unable to follow your instructions. They may need to be reassured that they have the ability to carry out the instructions. Reassurance tells others that we believe in them and their abilities. In effect, we are telling them that we think we can look ahead and predict that they will succeed.[6] We give them a pat on the back and help them to tackle the problem, whatever it might be.

For example, the mother just mentioned above may feel too inadequate to approach her son and discuss the matter of his smoking marijuana. She is afraid that she might break down or get so angry that she will just make matters worse. She needs reassurance so she can discuss this matter with her son. The counselor might reassure her by saying: "You have been able to talk about your son's problem with me in a relatively calm manner. I think you have enough composure and knowledge about this matter to sit down and discuss it with your son. I have confidence in your ability to do this."

GUIDELINES FOR GIVING REASSURANCE

Here are some guidelines for the use of reassurance.

1. Before giving reassurance, make sure it is well-founded. Giving unfounded reassurance can cause counselees to question whether you understand how they feel and what they are talking about.
2. Give reassurance only after you think you have a good estimate of the person's strengths and weaknesses and the demands of the situation.
3. Be confident in giving reassurance. Half-hearted or uncertain reassurance can undermine the counselee's self-confidence.
4. Use reassurance sparingly—only when you think it is really needed and is likely to be effective.

CONFRONTING

Confrontation is another means of influencing the way people think and act. Confrontation means pointing out discrepancies or distortions in the counselee's message and/or behavior. Confrontation is a responsible unmasking of discrepancies, distortions, games, and smoke screens that people use to hide both from self-understanding and from changing the way they act. It is "an invitation to examine some form of behavior that seems to be self-defeating or harmful to others and to change the behavior if it is found to be so."[7] Usually people who give conflicting messages have little or no awareness of what they are doing. At the appropriate time, it is the task of the counselor to bring to the person's awareness these conflicting messages. An example of this is the family man who says that he frequently works late and does not go home for dinner, but at the same time says that he enjoys being with his family. When he is questioned, he admits that he does not have to work overtime; he simply likes the quiet and freedom from distractions after everyone else has left the office. This man needs to face the discrepancy between his saying that he enjoys being with his wife and family and his needlessly working late and not coming home for dinner with his family. An example of a distortion might be the young woman who is single and tries to convince you of the glories of being single and independent but the tone of her voice and what you can read between the lines tells you that she is anything but convinced herself.

When we hear the word "confront," we frequently think of an attack. A confrontation is not an attack.[8] To be effective, a confrontation must be built on empathetic understanding, namely, the one confronting must have a good understanding of how people view their situation and how they feel about it. A confrontation should be an invitation to people to look within themselves and see that something is amiss. A confrontation should tell people that you care about them and you are trying to help them.

Before you try to confront a person you should have a good relationship with that person. The counselees should trust you and feel that you care about them and that you want to help them. Consequently, a confrontation is seldom used the first time you talk with a person. If you feel that you need to confront the person early on in your counseling relationship, the confrontation should be made tactfully and tentatively so that the person does not feel that you are attacking him or her.

Usually confronting another is not easy either for the counselor or the one being confronted because the confrontation often attempts to have the counselee face what the counselee does not want to face. Timing is all-important. You should prepare counselees for the confrontation. If the counselee becomes defensive, he or she will probably either deny the truth of what you have pointed out or argue against it; when this happens, it is better not to push your observation but come back to it when the counselee seems to be more receptive. Confrontation should be used sparingly and tactfully.

GUIDELINES FOR CONFRONTING

Here are some guidelines for confronting.

1. Confront only when you are genuinely concerned and care about the person.
2. Never use confrontation when you are frustrated or angry.
3. Confront only when you are convinced that you understand the person and the problem.
4. Rarely use confrontation at the first meeting with the person. Wait until you have established good rapport.
5. When confronting, use "I" rather than "you" statements. Say "I" think that you may be distorting the facts," rather than "You are distorting the facts." "You" statements are accusatory.
6. As much as possible, confront with facts and not opinions or inferences.
7. Make sure the person is ready to hear the confrontation. Lead into the confrontation.
8. Use confrontation sparingly—only when you think it could make a significant difference in the counselee's behavior or way of thinking.

LEADING

Counseling can be viewed as a form of teaching, whose purpose is to have another learn something new. Counseling as a form of teaching aims at having others learn new ways to deal with themselves, other people and their environment.[10] One method of teaching is called the Socratic method, after Socrates, the Greek philosopher, who used a series of well-formulated questions to lead his students to certain conclusions. When the Socratic method is used in counseling, it is called leading, which means that the counselor gets the counselee to accept the counselor's solution to a problem by using a series of questions. It should be noted that the counselor leads the counselee to a solution which is not the counselee's solution but the counselor's. For instance, a counselor may think that the counselee should quit her job. He asks a series of questions whose answers bring out how dissatisfied the counselee is with her job and by these questions causes her to accept the counselor's conclusion that she should quit. The counselor has led the counselee to a conclusion that may not be her own and which she may not want. This procedure is actually a disguised form of giving advice. Instead of telling the person outright what she should do, the counselor leads the person by a series of questions.

The Socratic method is the most direct form of leading a counselor can use. There is another form of leading where the counselee is not brought to accept the counselor's view. This form of leading is called refocusing the dialogue.[11] An example of refocusing is to be found in the interview where the counselor decides that it is essential for a married man to examine how he feels about his estranged wife and then tries to refocus the discussion by saying, "A little while back you said that you and your wife used to get into heated arguments. Could you tell me more about these arguments and especially how you felt about your wife at these times?" By using this procedure, the counselor causes the counselee to leave the topic he was discussing and return to something he has previously talked about.

GUIDELINES FOR LEADING

Here are some guidelines for the use of leading.

1. In using this skill, realize that you are taking over the direction the counseling will take. The solution is yours, not the counselee's.
2. Use the Socratic method only when you are convinced that counselees can resolve the problem in no other way.
3. Use leading as a means of refocusing the dialogue only when the topic under discussion has been exhausted and there is a value to return to a topic formerly discussed. Do not refocus when you are discussing another topic with the counselee.
4. When you use leading, keep clearly in mind where you want to lead the counselee.
5. Allow the counselee freedom to follow your lead.
6. After a counseling session, ask yourself whether you were leading the counselee. In your desire to find a quick solution, you may have led the counselee without realizing it.[12]

SUGGESTING AND GIVING ADVICE

Many people who seek pastoral counseling are looking for advice. Advice is telling someone how to act, what to do, or what not to do.[13] Suggestion is a type of advice, only milder in form. It is advice given in a tentative manner. Suggestion provides people with the counselor's considered opinion but leaves it up to them to accept or reject that opinion.[14] The counselee can take the suggestion or leave it, whereas advice is more demanding. In giving advice the counselor tells the counselee what he or she should do by saying something like this: "I think you should quit your job if that is the way your employer is treating you." When we as counselors give advice we are giving our opinion and telling others what we would do if we were in their position.

Advice can be given in different ways and for a variety of reasons. We can give advice directly by saying, "I think you should quit your job," or indirectly by putting the advice in the form of a question such as "I wonder if you have ever considered quitting your job." We can give advice because we are convinced that it is in the best interest of the individual to follow what we say, or because we think advice is what the person wants and we want to oblige, or finally because we have found that this is the least time-consuming way to handle an interview. Whether we are aware of it or not, most of us give advice in one form or another much more frequently than we realize.

There are times when we should give advice but these are few and far between. If we as counselors err, we err most frequently not because we have failed to give advice when it was needed but because we have succumbed to the urge to give advice when it would have been more beneficial to allow the person to decide with our assistance what he or she should do. Advice can actually harm people if it causes them to lose confidence in their ability to handle everyday problems and depend excessively on the advice of others.

When counselees directly seek advice by asking you what they should do, it is best to make sure that you thoroughly understand the difficulty or problem that prompted them to seek the advice before you decide whether or not to give the advice. If you immediately give your opinion you run the risk of giving poor advice because you may be giving advice based on inadequate data. You should have the person describe the whole situation as thoroughly as possible and then you will probably want to ask a number of questions to clarify those parts of the difficulty that you do not fully understand. You are now in a position to decide whether you want to give advice or not, and, if you want to give some advice, what advice you should give. The counselee's describing the problem in detail not only helps you to understand the problem but also helps the counselee to see the problem more clearly. Sometimes when people can clearly see what the problem is, they are able to think of a possible way or ways to solve the problem and then they do not need your advice.

If, however, you are still convinced that you need to give the counselees advice either because they do not have the intellectual resources to solve the problem on their own, or because they are too emotionally upset, or for some reason that seems valid to you, then it would be best to use a suggestion or advice put in the tentative form of a question, such as, "Have you ever thought of doing . . . ?" or "Could this be a possible answer to your difficulty?" Advice given in this form allows counselees to reject or amend what you have given them. People who truly need advice will most probably accept whatever you suggest because you are the expert and they realize that they are unable to decide what they should do or how they should act.

Whenever you give advice, you should realize that you may be taking away from other persons the responsibility of deciding for themselves what they should do or how they should act. If the advice does not help the counselee or makes the situation worse, the counselee is apt to blame you. Advice that does not help the person can undermine that person's trust and confidence in you as a counselor. It may even cause counselees not to seek help later on when they actually need it. Your giving advice also deprives counselees of the opportunity to make important decisions for themselves and grow as a consequence of making these decisions.

GUIDELINES FOR GIVING ADVICE

1. Give advice only when you are convinced that the persons cannot make a decision and/or act on their own.
2. Be sure that you fully understand the counselee's situation before you offer any kind of advice.
3. Give the advice in such a way as to leave room for the person to accept or reject the advice.
4. When you give advice, realize that advice can make people dependent on you and less likely to rely on their own resources.
5. Realize that you may be blamed if the advice does not work out.
6. Also realize that people can be hurt by advice, even when the advice is well-founded.[15]

SUMMARY

Besides attending and listening skills, there are influencing skills. Influencing skills are more direct and attempt to help counselees change the way they think, feel and act. The use of influencing skills presupposes that the counselor has listened carefully to what the counselee has said and manifests empathetic understanding.

We have considered the following influencing skills: (1) Giving Information, (2) Instruction, (3) Reassurance, (4) Confrontation, (5) Leading, and (6) Suggesting and Giving Advice.

Each of these procedures has a place in pastoral counseling, even if that place be quite limited. Proper timing and preparation are most important. Leading, suggesting and advice-giving should be used infrequently and then only when other procedures have failed or the counselor judges that leading, suggesting and advice-giving are the procedures of choice because of the counselee's limited intellectual resources or distraught emotional state.

8

===

Problem Solving

Many Christians are unable to cope with their problems, and so they seek counseling. They are not looking for psychological counseling; they are looking for pastoral counseling. They want to find a way to cope with their situation that takes into consideration their Christian commitment and may even use this commitment to find a solution to their problem.

BEGINNING

Counseling begins with the first contact, whether this is on the telephone, in a home, outside a church, or in an office. First impressions that are made at these times often set the way the person relates to the counselor. If counselees see the counselor as a warm, interested person, they are much more likely to discuss freely their problem. On the other hand, if the counselor seems distracted, distant, or not interested, they will probably be hesitant to talk about what is troubling them.

Most seeking pastoral counseling come on their own. They realize they have a problem and need help. Usually they are unable to cope with a difficult situation. Your first task is to try to understand the situation in all its details and ramifications. You should try to look at the situation as the counselee sees it, mindful that the counselee may see a problem in a very different way from you. For instance, an elderly woman who lives alone and whose twelve year old dog has recently died seeks help because of a persistent urge to commit suicide. She sees no reason for living any longer. For some counselors, the desire to end one's life because a dog died borders on the ridiculous, but for this woman the dog was her only and constant companion for many years. Its death means one thing to the counselor, and quite another to the woman. To take the dog's death lightly or dismiss it as not the real reason for the suicidal thoughts would probably negate any chance of your helping this woman.

With a minimum of encouragement most people will begin spontaneously to explain why they are seeking help. You need only listen and respond in such a way as to indicate that you are interested and trying to understand what is going on in the counselee's life. If, however, the counselee has trouble getting started, it is sometimes helpful to use an open-ended question, such as, "How did you happen to come today?" or "What would you like to talk about today?"

Once you think you have a fairly clear picture of the problem and what is going on in the person's life, it is good to summarize what you have heard so far. This summary ties together the main elements of what the person has said and it also serves as a check for you and the counselee if you heard correctly and understood what was said. A well-phrased summary often underlines the essential elements of the problem for the counselee.[1]

KEEPING THE DISCUSSION FOCUSED

Some people cannot describe their difficulties in an ordered, logical fashion. They tend to drift from one topic to another. If they are allowed to continue along this path, the counselor often ends up wondering what is the central problem and then is unable to move the counselee in the direction of a solution. Moreover, no one topic is fully examined, and often little is gained from the session. Your task is to get the person to concentrate on one central problem, preferably the one he or she sees as the most important, and then define this problem fully and in concrete terms.[2] Asking for specific examples helps to clarify the problem.

Sometimes people give a pseudo-problem. They are often testing the waters to make sure that you as counselor can be trusted. Your reaction determines whether the counselee talks about the real reason that brought him or her to counseling or not. If you show empathetic understanding, and do not jump quickly to advice-giving and problem solving, the odds are that the counselee will begin to talk about the real problem. If you try to tell the person what she should do, she may reject the advice, and say, "Yes but I tried that and it did not work," or she may simply ignore the advice. On occasion, you may have to be directive and make the counselee settle on one main problem.

Some people who seek help do not know what is wrong. They just know that they are unhappy and dissatisfied with life. They may place the blame on some vague cause like their lack of faith or their failure to practice their religion, saying, "If I were a better Catholic, I would not have all this trouble." In this case, you need to find out how long they have been unhappy, and then whether there have been any recent changes in their lives that might have precipitated their depressed state. You probably will have to use specific closed-questions to get this information.[3] Once specific causes for unhappiness have surfaced, the counselee needs to examine these causes more fully and then, if they appear to be valid, to cope with them.

In the beginning, your main task is to help the counselee decide what is the problem, and then spell it out in detail.[4] At first people usually present a problem situation on a surface level, and need encouragement to go more in depth. This means that they need to see what effect the problem is having on them and how they feel about it, who else is being influenced and how, and what are its consequences. Usually the counselee will spontaneously offer much of this information, but often some aspects are overlooked. A few well formulated questions bring the overlooked matter to their attention.

EXPECTATIONS

People come with a variety of expectations. These expectations can determine the ultimate success or failure of the counseling. If their expectations are not met they are apt to leave the session disappointed, and possibly not return. Thus it is important to find out as soon as possible what the person hopes to gain from the contact.[5]

If you happen to be a priest or minister, sister or brother, some will see you as an authority figure with special powers. They expect you to give them sound advice, or even solve their problem for them. For instance, a woman with a deteriorating marriage may expect you to talk to her husband and get him to change what she considers irresponsible behavior. If you try to focus on her part in the marriage conflict, and what she can do to improve the situation, this woman may become upset and break off the counseling. If you are going to help her, it is important to know her expectations and, if necessary, indicate to her that they are unrealistic. Counseling and psychotherapy are an accepted part of middle-class America. Through reading and conversation with friends who have had counseling, most know what is expected. The same is not true among the lower class and some minority groups.[6] Many of these people expect to be interviewed, and then told what they should do. When such individuals seek assistance from a counselor in pastoral ministry, they frequently must be taught how to be a counselee. If they are not and their expectations are not met, they may become frustrated and stop coming for counseling.

Some people have unrealistic expectations. They were helped before, so they will be helped again. All they have to do is talk to a priest or nun, and the talking itself will do the job. They fail to realize that they themselves must take some specific steps to bring about change, either in themselves or in their environment. Others put their total confidence in the pastoral counselor, whom they look upon as having powers ordinary counselors do not have. If they just follow the advice, the problem, whatever it might be, will be solved. However, it should be noted that when the advice does not work, especially if this happens several times, these people become disillusioned, and are apt not to seek help the next time they need it.

ESTABLISHING GOALS

Once the problem is clearly defined and expectations established, the next step is to determine the goals. The goals are a clear statement of what the person wants to do concretely and specifically to handle the problem situation or some part of it.[7] The goal or goals tell what the counseling is supposed to accomplish and where it is going. Discussing a problem, even at great length, seldom solves the problem. Usually the person needs to take some kind of action steps. The purpose of counseling is to help the person decide what steps to take. Let us take the case of a twenty-seven year old woman married four years and with one child. She comes seeking help in coping with her husband's drinking, which she considers excessive. She says he is considerate and loving except when he is drinking. When she has tried to talk with him about this problem, he has become angry, and occasionally abusive. She tells you that his father was an alcoholic, and she is afraid that he will also become an alcoholic. In this case, the goal of the counseling would be to help this woman find some way of getting her husband to face up to the potential danger of continuing his present drinking habit.

If at all possible, the goal should be what the counselee wants. It should not be one decided upon by the counselor, and then "pushed on" the counselee. Frequently, this means that the goal will have to be discussed with the counselee. It is essential that counselees "own" the goal or goals, namely that they look upon them as their own, and not those of the counselor.[8] Thus, this woman would have to want to find a way of approaching her husband, and want it very much, before this would be a viable goal. If she were pressured into getting his best friend to discuss the matter with him, but she really did not believe that this would help, the odds are that she would never implement the goal.

The goals should be clear and specific.[9] In some way the counselee should be able to visualize the outcome when the action steps are taken. The results of the actions should be observable, and even measurable, as well as spelled out in detail. In the case of this woman, a possible goal might be to try to relate better with her husband so that eventually she can discuss the drinking problem with him without his becoming angry, but this goal is too vague and abstract. A clear, specific goal would be for her to settle on concrete ways of improving their relationship, such as going bowling with him, which he likes, and afterward have a meal together, at which time they could talk about personal matters. At the appropriate time, she could calmly and without nagging bring up the excessive drinking and the possibility of his discussing it with an expert in the field of alcohol abuse.

The goal should be realistic, which means that the person should have resources to accomplish the goal, external circumstances do not get in the way of realizing the goal, and the cost is not too high.[10] If this woman is unable to discuss the topic of drinking because of her negative bias against all drinking, any goal which includes her talking about this with her husband would probably not be viable. Likewise, having her husband see an expert in the field of alcohol abuse when there is no such person available would not be a viable goal. And, finally, for her to continue arguing with her husband to stop drinking, even when he reacts with anger and verbal abuse, is too costly. It could end in separation or divorce.

GATHERING MORE INFORMATION

Additional information about the person's social and environmental situation is sometimes needed, so as to list possible courses of action. This usually can be done by asking a series of closed questions. Care, however, should be taken lest you give the impression that you are trying to figure out what has gone wrong, and then intend to tell the person what he or she should do, much like a physician who diagnoses and prescribes a treatment. If counselees get this impression, they come to expect you to solve their problem for them, and lose sight of the essential element of counseling, namely that counselors try to help counselees help themselves.

If you make use of appropriate counseling skills, especially the skill of empathetic understanding, most people will usually give almost all the needed information without your asking questions. Sometimes, however, counselees omit an important element, such as whether they are married, the number of children they have, or the type of work they do. These facts can sometimes determine whether a possible course of action is viable. For instance, there is little possibility of the husband who is drinking excessively undergoing treatment in an expensive alcohol rehabilitation program if he has a low paying job and his health insurance does not cover such a program. If his wife never told you about these facts, useless time could be spent discussing a rehabilitation program as a viable option.

Questioning for added information should only be used after counselees have described the situation that prompted them to come for help, and then the questions should be used to complete the picture. There is a tendency among counselors, particularly those who are inexperienced, to overuse questioning.[11] When the dialogue begins to lag, some counselors become anxious, lest there be a period of silence with their not knowing what to say, and so they automatically begin asking questions, which often are simply fillers and go nowhere. They forget that the purpose of asking questions is to get needed information. When questions are used because the counselor does not know what to say, they are pointless and can undermine the counseling process.

CONSIDERING COURSES OF ACTION

All that has gone before sets the stage for the next step, namely helping the person figure out a way to solve the problem. Once the problem is clearly defined and the goals established, often the dialogue spontaneously begins to focus on possible ways the counselee might cope with the situation.

Usually there are several courses of action, which the counselee needs to look at and evaluate.[12] Let us consider some possible courses of action the woman whose husband is drinking excessively might take: (1) She might continue trying to discuss the matter with her husband, but not in an angry, nagging way and try to get him to see an expert in alcohol rehabilitation. (2) She might get his best friend to talk with him about his drinking. (3) She might get him to see his pastor. (4) She might join Al-Anon and see if this helps her to cope with the problem. These are all possible action steps she could take, with one being more likely to succeed than the others.

In formulating possible courses of action, you should first try to get the counselee to give the way she sees that the problem could be solved, and then, if necessary, you can suggest other possibilities, but be careful to give these merely as suggestions. People have a tendency to see you as an expert, and take what you suggest as more valid and likely to succeed than the course of action they propose, which may or may not be true.

One way of generating possible solutions to the problem is to ask the person if she has ever been in a similar situation before such as having to cope with an alcoholic parent. If the response is affirmative, then ask what she did and finally whether she thinks the same way of acting would work in the present situation.

Sometimes people find it difficult to think of possible courses of action. When you ask them whether they have thought of any, they may respond: "If I had, I would not be here," or "I have tried everything I can think of but nothing seems to work." In such cases, it may be necessary to ask the person to brainstorm any possibility, even those that do not seem likely to succeed. Some people have a negative attitude; they immediately think of all the reasons why a particular action step will not succeed, and so they never propose any. If the counselee is unable to think of any ways to handle the situation, then you might give some suggestions by saying "Have you ever thought of . . . ?" If the person immediately refutes all your suggestions, it may be that the counselee really does not want to find a solution, at least not at the present time or at the price it will cost.

EVALUATING COURSES OF ACTION

Once three or four possible courses of actions have been formulated, the next step is to summarize these. If you were counseling the woman whose husband drinks excessively, you might say, "There seem to be three possible courses you could take in dealing with your husband's excessive drinking. First, you could wait for what you consider the right time and then try to talk about it again with him, calmly and without nagging, and try to get him to see an expert; or another possibility is to get his best friend to talk with him about his drinking; or finally you could join Al-Anon and see if you get any help from this organization in handling this problem." With fairly bright people, it is often helpful to ask them to summarize the possible ways of solving the problem. If they can summarize the possible action steps, then you can be relatively sure that they understand them. The summary gives counselees a clearer picture of what is possible and generates hope since they can then see that there are possible ways of solving the problem, some of which they may not have thought of before.

The next step is to go back and consider with the counselee each possible way of handling the situation by asking the counselee what is in favor of the particular solution and then what are its limitations or drawbacks.[12] In considering what favors and what is against adopting a particular solution, most counselees are able to give a list of several reasons for trying the solution and then a similar list against it. More often than not, there are more reasons in one list than in the other, which may become the basis for a later decision. The counselee then compares the list of reasons favoring the possible solution with the list of reasons against it, notes whether the list of reasons favoring the solution is longer and more impressive than the list opposing it or vice versa, and determines which list of reasons seems to have the greater weight. After considering at some length what is in favor and what is against a possible solution, most counselees are able to make the decision to accept or reject the way of handling the problem as a likely solution, which then should be compared with the other two or three possible ways of handling the problem, once they have been evaluated. The next step is to ask the person to consider the second possible solution and the same process is repeated; then the third possible solution, etc. Frequently, after discussing all three or four possible solutions in this manner, one stands out as the best and the most likely to succeed. In this case, it is relatively easy for the counselee to decide on which one to follow.

Sometimes two possible ways of handling the problem seem equally good. If they are not incompatible, the counselee might be able to make use of both ways. For instance, the woman whose husband is drinking excessively might decide to join Al-Anon and also, after being a member for a time, try to discuss the matter again with her husband and try to get him to see an expert. If they are incompatible, then the counselee should weigh again the relative merits of each and decide which has the greater possibility of succeeding.

CRITERIA FOR ACCEPTING OR REJECTING A POSSIBLE SOLUTION

The decision to accept one way of trying to solve a problem over the others is based on these factors: (1) the number of reasons why the person should use the solution are more numerous and weighty than the reasons for the other possible solutions and the reasons opposed to it are fewer and less weighty; (2) the use of this way of handling the problem is more likely to accomplish the established goals of the counseling; (3) the chances of the way succeeding are greater than the other ways; (4) the solution is in agreement with the faith and Christian values of the counselee whereas some of the other proposed solutions may not be.

Usually the way of handling the problem that stands out as most likely to succeed is the one which has the largest number of reasons that favor accepting it. This is especially true if the reasons are weighty ones. A solution that has a large number of reasons for not accepting it is very likely to be disregarded in favor of one of the other ways.

If a way of solving the problem is to be considered a valid way, it must be one which achieves the specified goal of the counseling. For example, in the case of the woman whose husband engages in excessive drinking, the way of handling the problem that she decides to follow must eventually assist her to get her husband to examine his pattern of drinking and make whatever changes in his drinking that he sees are needed. If the way this woman decides to follow does not achieve this goal, then this way of handling the problem obviously is not as good as one of the other ways which does.

Most counselees place great weight on whether they think the way of handling the problem will succeed or not. If it appears that one way is most likely to bring results, then the counselee is likely to choose it, even though another way of solving the problem may have more reasons in favor of accepting it. The reasons why the counselee thinks the solution is more apt to succeed is often linked to past experience. Counselees may have found that when they have been in a similar situation and used this type of a solution, it has usually worked, and so they are inclined to use it again.

In pastoral counseling the faith and values of the counselee play an important role. If the way of handling a problem is incompatible with the person's Christian faith and values, this way is not a valid solution to the problem and should be rejected. For example, divorce and remarriage is not an acceptable solution for the woman mentioned above because such a solution is incompatible with her Christian faith and values. Moreover, Christian faith is meant to be a dynamic force in our lives. It can be the main force that gives a person strength to put into action the way of solving a problem that the person has chosen. Her faith and appreciation of marriage as a sacrament and permanent commitment might be the one thing that motivates this woman to do everything possible to improve her relationship with her husband so that she can talk with him about his drinking in a constructive way, which is something she probably finds very difficult because she is so emotionally involved in the problem.

In evaluating possible ways of handling a problem, faith and religious values often enter into the picture. The solution of a Christian can radically differ from that of the non-believer. Faith adds a new dimension to many of our actions, which comes into play in the evaluation stage. For instance, the committed Christian values human life wherever he or she sees it. If that person happens to be a pregnant unmarried teenager, her view of abortion is likely to be quite different from that of the girl who has no commitment to Christianity. When she is faced with the task of formulating possible ways of handling her problem, abortion is contrary to her faith and values, and therefore is not a viable option.

Sometimes the counselor in pastoral ministry will have to help counselees clarify what they hold as Christians so that they can use these positions and values in evaluating possible courses of action. This process differentiates pastoral counseling from psychological counseling. The pastoral counselor represents the Church and is called to make others aware of Christ's message, not only in the pulpit and the classroom but also in the counseling office.

After weighing the merits and deficiencies of each possible way of handling the problem, the counselees are asked to decide on the one which seems best to them and commensurate with their faith and Christian value system.

IMPLEMENTING THE DECISION

Once the decision is made the next thing to do is to get the person to decide on what steps must be taken to implement the decision.[13] Many people make decisions but never act on them. Deciding on a plan of action greatly enhances the possibility of the counselee's implementing a recently made decision. Counselees need to settle on when, where, and how they intend to implement their decision. For example, let us say that the woman we have been considering decides that she would like to join Al-Anon. In helping her implement her decision, you would have to ask her if she has any familiarity with Al-Anon and knows how to contact them. If she does, then you would ask her when it would be convenient for her to call the local Al-Anon chapter and find out what she must do to join. It would be helpful if you could get her to settle on a definite time she would make the call, such as this afternoon or tomorrow morning. You should also ask her about the days she is free to attend the meetings and how she will get to the meetings. If counselees know that they must return to report on their progress in implementing the decision they have made, they are even more likely to follow through on the action step.

One should not expect always to follow exactly the problem-solving plan we have just given, step by step from beginning to the end. One step may occur simultaneously with another; one or other step may be omitted; or the counselee may simply wish to define the problem with no thought of finding a solution. Some counselees are looking for a little emotional support so as to live with an impossible situation, in which case the problem-solving technique would not apply.

The value of the problem-solving technique is its giving the counselor an orderly format that gives the counseling direction. When people see that you are following a technique that seems to be going somewhere, their confidence in your ability increases, and they are apt to be more cooperative. With some it is helpful to spell out the essential elements of the technique at the beginning. This is especially true with people who like order and structure.

Like any counseling technique, problem-solving needs to be tailored to the needs of the counselee. Counseling is sometimes said to be an art. It is an art to know when to apply and when not to apply a technique. For people with distressing problems which they seem unable to handle, the problem-solving technique can be most helpful.

It has an added value inasmuch as it can give counselees a systematic way of handling future problems. Once people learn the process by working through it several times, they are usually able later to apply it without the help of a counselor. The problem-solving technique then becomes a learned skill that can be used over and over again.

SUMMARY

The problem-solving technique involves the following steps:

1. Define the central problem that prompted the person to seek counseling.

2. Establish the goals: what does the person hope to achieve as a result of the counseling?
3. Establish possible courses of action the counselee could take to solve the problem.
4. Evaluate what is in favor of and what is opposed to each course of action based on achieving the goal of the counseling, likelihood of success, and the person's Christian faith and values.
5. Get the counselee to decide on one course of action.
6. Devise a plan to implement this course of action.
7. Arrange for the person to return and report on progress in implementing the decided upon course of action.

The above-mentioned plan does not have to be followed rigidly. There may be an overlap between steps. After considering the counselee's situation, you may want to omit one or other step. The plan gives structure and direction to your counseling which can be most helpful for some people.

9

Supportive Measures

For some problems there are no solutions or at least not for the present. Yet many people seek counseling when confronted with a problem they know they cannot solve. Some examples of problems that do not seem to have an immediate solution are the man with an aged mother who is a disruptive force in his home but not so debilitated as to need care in a home for the aged or the woman with an alcoholic husband who has completed several rehabilitation programs but to no avail and who does not want to leave him after many years of married life. Even though these people realize that there is no acceptable solution to their problem, they still come to a pastoral counselor for help, and may even come several times.

There are times in the lives of all of us when pressures and stresses seem overwhelming. The opportunity to talk about these pressures and stresses with an interested and caring person often gives us a different perspective and we come to realize that we are not as overwhelmed as we thought we were; all that we need is some understanding and encouragement.

SUPPORTIVE THERAPY

In psychotherapy there is a process called supportive therapy whose purpose is to assist clients over a particularly difficult period by giving them someone to lean on for a time. The process is akin to giving a cane to a man with a sprained ankle so he does not have to put his full weight on the ankle until it is better. The cane gives additional support and allows sprained muscles to rehabilitate themselves more easily. Counselors in pastoral ministry make use of something similar to supportive therapy when they allow counselees to lean on them during a particularly stressful period, such as when a loved one dies, a marriage breaks up, or a job is lost. The purpose of the counseling is not to help the person solve a problem but simply to offer emotional support. Offering this support allows the counselees time to recoup their inner strength and reestablish lost self-confidence.

Enelow defines supportive therapy as "any action on the part of the counselor that communicates interest in, liking for, understanding of, and helps give the person a feeling of security."[1] Your caring attitude toward the people you counsel tells them that they can depend upon you to help them through a particularly distressing time and that they are not alone in their struggle. Your calm, confident manner gives your counselees confidence that they will be able to handle their problems, even though they may not clearly see how.

The major goals of supportive therapy are: (1) to reduce high levels of negative emotions, such as anger and fear, (2) to strengthen controls on behavior and lessen the risk of impulsive and ill-advised actions, and (3) to lessen the feeling of anxiety and restore some peace of mind.[2] Supportive therapy aims at helping people ventilate their emotions, especially feelings of frustration and anger, and then cope as best they can with a situation for which there seems to be no immediate solution.

WHY DO SUPPORTIVE MEASURES HELP PEOPLE?

1. They allow people to see that another person values their intrinsic worth at a time when they are beginning to doubt their own worth.
2. They reaffirm and strengthen the person's sense of worth.
3. They reduce anxiety and develop a sense of security.
4. They lessen feelings of aloneness and isolation.
5. They give counselees a feeling of hope and keep them from withdrawing from life.
6. They give people permission to feel as they do and not feel guilty about it.
7. They lessen the possibility of counselees accepting ill-advised solutions.

Unless supportive efforts spring from a genuine concern on the part of the counselor, they will appear forced and artificial. If you do not feel concern for the counselee, you cannot successfully fake it. Enelow says: "A supportive attitude is a compound of a number of elements, notably: 1) genuine interest and concern for the patient; 2) a feeling of warmth and friendliness toward the patient; 3) a desire to be helpful; and 4) maintenance of sufficient reserve, so that the therapist remains clearly aware that he is engaging in a helping relation."[3]

WHAT DO COUNSELORS DO TO BE SUPPORTIVE?

1. They manifest warmth and concern but at the same time maintain an appropriate reserve.
2. They listen attentively and are empathetic.
3. They manifest confidence in their own ability as counselors.

4. They are encouraging and take a positive stance in regard to what distresses the person.
5. They encourage the person to ventilate his or her feelings and emotions, especially the negative ones, neither condemning in any way nor trying to cut short emotional outbursts of anger and hurt.
6. They gradually try to bring the person to a new perspective and gain strength from his or her faith.

Often the way counselors conduct themselves can indicate a supportive attitude. A friendly smile or the use of a first name demonstrates warmth and caring. A simple but sincere greeting such as "How are you today?" or "Did you have a good vacation?" shows personal interest. A firm handshake or a hand on the shoulder as the person leaves is affirming. A genial comment about what interests the counselee shows personal concern for the counselee as an individual. Affirming the counselee by saying "You are doing the right thing by acting that way" bolsters lagging self-confidence. People are strengthened when an expert agrees with their decision or way of acting.

"Supportive psychotherapy uses such techniques as a warm, friendly, strong leadership; a gratification of dependency needs if it can be done without evoking undue shame; support in the development of legitimate dependence; help in the development of hobbies and of pleasurable but non-destructive sublimation; adequate rest and diversion; the removal of excessive strain if that is a productive step. It uses those techniques that may make the patient feel more secure, accepted, protected, encouraged, safe, or less anxious and less alone."[4] As supportive therapy is a valuable tool for psychiatrists and psychologists, so too it can be for counselors in pastoral ministry. It is quite likely that counselors in pastoral ministry frequently use supportive measures by actively using their position in the Church to encourage and inspire people to continue to struggle with what seems overwhelming to them.

Sometimes your presence as a representative of the Church is all that is needed. Little more is asked of you than that you listen and try to understand what the person is going through. Your actions tell the person that you and the Church care about them. What you say may have little impact because the person is too distracted to give it much reflection. What matters is how you say it; whether it is genuine, sincere and shows that you care. Your attentive listening can be most supportive, deeply appreciated, and a genuine act of charity.

GRIEF COUNSELING

Two situations which call for supportive measures and are frequently encountered in pastoral ministry are the death of a loved one and a divorce. To be supportive the counselor needs to understand what people experience when they suffer a loss through either death or a divorce. We all tend to want to change grief and sadness to joy and happiness. None of us likes to sit with a crying person. We want and often try to do something to make the person feel better, whereas what the person actually needs most is to experience the sadness and grief and work through it. In the long run, trying to cheer people up or distract them is usually not being helpful. The grieving person needs to face the loss and experience all the emotions that accompany it.

Grief is emotional pain due to loss or deprivation. The person who experiences the death of a loved one usually goes through three stages of mourning which can overlap or be arrested at one or other stage.[5] The important thing is to understand what the bereaved is experiencing rather than the sequence. "The first stage consists of shock, protest, anger and disbelief. The person cannot comprehend what has happened."[6] Such persons may feel numb, empty, dazed, and confused, and may even lash out at God in anger, saying: "Why did God take her? She was so young. Why didn't God take the old man who goes to church every morning?" Or the anger may be leveled at the doctor, themselves or even the deceased person. For some people the finality of death is not accepted. They look for the deceased to return. All these reactions have a purpose; they serve as a barrier against overwhelming grief and sorrow, which can last for several days and then give way to an all-encompassing sorrow that is expressed through extended periods of crying.

The second stage of normal bereavement begins a couple of weeks after the funeral services when the individual must confront the reality of daily living without the other person. Three distinct behavior patterns are characteristic of this phase. First, the bereaved engages in obsessional reviewing by dwelling on one or several of the scenes associated with the death. Such persons berate themselves with thoughts like, "If I had only made him wear his seat belt!" or "If I had only made her go to the doctor earlier!" With time the futility of this reviewing is recognized and the death is accepted. The second way of acting is to search for the meaning of the death. The bereaved wants to know why it had to happen and asks, "Why did she have to die?" Some people can accept that it was God's will; others never find a satisfactory answer. The final experience of the bereaved is the most intriguing; it is a process best described as searching for the deceased. A number of activities that they previously shared evoke an imagined presence of the deceased. For example, watching television may cause the bereaved to feel that the departed one is present and sharing the experience of watching television with them.

Obsessional reviewing, the search for an understanding of the death, and the search for the presence of the deceased tend to decrease with time. For most individuals functional stability returns within a few months after the death; many fully recover by the end of the first year.

The third and last stage in the sequence of bereavement is recovery. The recovery stage is often preceded by a conscious decision by the bereaved that dwelling on the past is fruitless and that life must now move on. Eventually most people reenter the social world; some find it difficult because they see themselves assigned to a peripheral status; the widow or widower will say, "My married friends do not want to see me because I am single. We no longer have anything in common." Sometimes new relationships have to be established. It is not unusual, however, for the bereaved to come out of the experience a stronger person: one reason being that he or she can take pride in having dealt with and survived a devastating event and another that new daily living skills have been acquired such as learning how to manage household finances or how to cook, each of which enhances self-esteem. The main task of the pastoral counselor in dealing with grieving people is to be supportive and assist them as they pass through the various stages of bereavement.

MORBID GRIEF

Morbid grief reactions are not qualitatively different from normal grief reactions; they differ only in intensity and duration. In his study of bereavement, Lindemann observed that the most striking feature of an abnormal grief reaction is the delay of the emotional response for several weeks or even months.[7] During this period of delay the bereaved individual exhibits a sense of well-being, and even zest, but as a result of internalizing the grief response the period of apparent calm is followed by profound changes in behavior, including intense hostility toward special individuals, irritability with relatives and friends, and an inability to initiate any activity without the urging of someone else. These individuals may behave in ways detrimental to their social and economic well-being; for example, they may alienate themselves from their closest friends or they may give away most of their possessions.

The following is a case history of an abnormal grief reaction which called for more than ordinary supportive measures by a pastoral counselor.

John, aged forty-one, a high school teacher whose wife had died sixteen months ago, came to the parish rectory to seek help. After saying that he was in terrible shape and did not know what to do, he started to cry. Gradually and with great difficulty, he was able to tell how his wife died of cancer well over a year ago. John and his wife were married for twenty years and were deeply in love with each other. Almost everything they did, they did together. The center of their attention and activity was a beautiful home and garden, much of which was the result of their own work. All through his wife's long illness he was at her side; he was optimistic that she would eventually recover. When she finally gave up the struggle and died, he could not believe that she was really gone. John held up well during the period of the funeral but a few days later he went into a deep depression from which he never recovered. He took a leave of absence from work and withdrew from all social contacts. His teenaged children had to take care of him rather than he care for them. He spent his time keeping the house and garden exactly as it was when his wife was alive, even to the point of planting only the flowers she liked and in the spots where she would have planted them.

A few months ago he decided that his children needed a mother and that he should do something to pull himself together. He and his deceased wife had been close friends with a woman whose husband had died a number of years before, leaving her with two small children. He thought that she would make a good wife and mother for his children and that he could be a father to her children. He visited her several times and then suggested that they get married, to which she eventually agreed. After the wedding John quickly discovered that he was repulsed by any signs of affection from his new wife and that they were unable to have intercourse. The new wife was understanding but he felt shattered, humiliated and more depressed than ever. It was at this point that John sought help from a counselor in pastoral ministry.

This man manifests many signs of the first and second stage of grieving. His reactions are morbid because he continued in these stages, even though his wife had been dead well over a year. At this point supportive measures were not enough; he needed psychotherapy to move him into the recovery stage. If he had talked several times with a pastoral counselor shortly after the death of his wife, it is likely that he would have passed through the normal stages of grieving and his grief reaction may not have become morbid.

HELPING THE BEREAVED

The following are some steps you can take in trying to help the bereaved.

1. Encourage the bereaved to tell you what happened at the death of the loved one—how he or she reacted, how the family members reacted and what they said. Allow the person to express shock, protest, anger, and to cry.
2. Encourage the person to talk about the past relationship with the deceased, to talk about the past joys and sorrows.

3. Listen for indications of denial but realize that the person needs to use denial to lessen the pain of loss.
4. Hear and acknowledge feelings of sadness, guilt, and anger.
5. Listen for indications of previous losses or separations, how the person coped with these, and whether there was a satisfactory closure or whether there is still unfinished business which increases the reaction to the present loss.
6. Be aware of the personal strengths, such as good self-understanding or openness to his or her own feelings and help the person use these strengths.
7. In the case of normal grief, assure the person that what he or she is experiencing is normal and that he or she is not going insane.[8]

All of these measures are supportive. They allow bereaved people to gather together their resources and work through their grief reaction in a normal way. As a consequence of this support, they may not only return to a normal state of well-being but even become stronger.

DIVORCE

Divorce and separation like death involves a loss. Just as there is a period of mourning over the death of someone we love, so also is there one when a divorce occurs. To help newly divorced or separated people, counselors in pastoral ministry need to understand what the newly divorced or separated are experiencing and then help them work through the stages of mourning.

Even though a number of people seems to look upon a divorce as a freeing and positive experience, research shows that marital disruption almost uniformly gives rise to distress, irrespective of the quality of the marriage.[9] Once the separation is seen as final, the person is likely to feel sad, depressed, lonely, isolated, angry, and guilty.

The sadness is due to the loss of one's very self. After years of married life, individuals come to accept being married as an integral part of their personality. By a divorce this part of themselves is lost, which produces sadness and depression. "There persists after the end of most marriages, whether they are happy or unhappy, whether their disruption has been sought or not, a sense of bonding to the spouse. Some feel anxious, fearful, or terrified both when contemplating a prospective separation from the spouse and when experiencing the spouse's absence. Others feel drawn to the spouse after separation, even though they may have decided against a continued relationship with the spouse."[10] The pining seems to fade as time passes and there is no contact with the former spouse.

Loneliness and a feeling of isolation are further reactions to separation. "Loneliness is fraught with a lot of anxiety and fear. One of the basic fears with which we are all confronted when we are lonely is whether or not we are genuinely acceptable to other people."[11] If the divorced person has to live alone, the absence of the spouse and a sense of isolation can be overpowering.

Among recently divorced people anger is a predominant reaction, which is especially true if the divorce was unwanted or the former spouse was unfaithful. "Separating spouses may be angry with each other not only because they blame each other for their distress but also because of a genuine conflict in interests. Such conflicts are most likely to occur in relation to property division, support payments, custody of children and visitation."[12] There are often accusations and counter-accusations, escalating the anger to the point where one spouse may actually fantasize harming or even killing the other.

Guilt is still another reaction. There is a tendency to review the past and ask how they could have acted differently and thus averted the final separation. Even when they are angry with the former spouse, some people blame themselves for the disintegration of the marriage. Guilt lowers one's sense of personal worth; excessive guilt can bring on a depression.

STAGES IN GETTING A DIVORCE

There are four stages in the process of getting a divorce: (1) the predivorce decision period, (2) the decision period, (3) the period of mourning, and (4) the period of reestablishing equilibrium. Counselors in pastoral ministry may enter the process at any one of these stages, but they more often enter it at the mourning stage because that is the stage when people most often seek help. When marriage counseling begins during the first two stages, the use of a problem solving technique is often helpful. Supportive measures are also appropriate.

During the stage that precedes the decision to separate or get a divorce there is a growing dissatisfaction with the marriage, which is often felt more by one party than the other. Sometimes one party is only vaguely aware that there is something amiss in the relationship and may accept this fact as just part of married life, while the other party has already decided to get a divorce. When the announcement is made, it comes as a surprise and shock. In the majority of cases, however, both partners are aware of a gradual corrosion of the relationship and may make an effort to reestablish the relationship. It might be noted that this is the point in the deterioration of a marriage where counseling is the most effective. Often arguments and fights are interspersed during this time with attempts at reconciliation, but what one spouse says to the other in the heat of anger can sometimes cause irreparable damage.

The second stage is the period of making a decision which is marked by a firm decision by at least one of the partners to separate or get a divorce. The final decision may bring a sense of relief but there is usually considerable anxiety about being able to live alone as a single person. The decision to get a divorce also introduces new issues, such as the care and support of the children and the division of common property, which can provoke heated arguments and lead to mutual animosity. Divorce mediation can help both parties to handle child custody and the division of the property amicably. In divorce mediation a professional counselor tries to help the parties agree on a final settlement without going to court for a decision on these matters.

The next stage is a period of mourning which begins once a separation has taken place, when the papers for a court hearing are served, or after the divorce is finally granted. At this time the person experiences depression and loneliness. If the person is a Catholic and feels that marriage is for life with no opportunity for remarriage, he or she may feel trapped in the unwanted single state. At this stage many people experience a sense of failure which gives way to self-recrimination and ruminating about what they could have done to save the marriage. As a consequence, their self-esteem and self-worth is at a low level.[13] Some people lose all self-confidence in their ability to relate to others and withdraw from social contacts. Even when former spouses do not withdraw from social contacts, they still feel out of place and unwanted by their married friends. Moreover, they find that their friends are often put in the position where they have to side with one or other party in the divorce; often they end up also mourning the loss of a number of friends.[14] The return of anger toward the former spouse usually marks the end of the period of mourning.

Recovery is the final stage, which usually begins when the divorced parties are able to put the broken marriage behind them and begin to establish a new life-style as a divorced person, making new friends, and developing new interests. They may even begin to experience an inner freedom which they never had in the married state. They no longer ruminate about the past. They discover they can be at ease living alone; the blame for the divorce is no longer entirely theirs or the former spouse's; they can accept their part in causing the divorce and move on. They begin to think about the future. Their self-confidence and self-esteem is reestablished, and may even be increased by the divorce.

STEPS TO HELP PEOPLE SEPARATING OR GETTING A DIVORCE

The following are steps that may be taken to assist people who are contemplating or have decided upon separation or divorce.

1. Allow the person to express negative feelings, such as anger, a sense of failure, guilt, self-recrimination, sadness and loneliness.
2. Encourage the person to talk about the lost marriage relationship and the divorce process.
3. Determine how severe is the sense of loss and how disruptive is the divorce to one's life-style.
4. Assist the person to accept the finality of the separation when it is obvious that the other party has no intention of reestablishing the relationship.
5. Help the person then understand the causes of the separation or divorce, both one's own and the other party's contribution.
6. Address various fears about the future, both realistic and unrealistic.

Initially the goal of the process should be supportive

rather than confrontive. The person should feel that you are on his or her side. Challenging or contesting the validity of statements the person makes may increase emotional distress and alienate the person. As his or her negative and disruptive emotions subside, you can tentatively suggest other ways of looking at past incidents that led to the separation or divorce.

SUMMARY

Supportive measures can be useful in pastoral counseling. By showing interest, concern, understanding, acceptance, and a desire to help, counselors indicate to counselees that they esteem them and can be depended upon in a time of need. Supportive measures help people continue to struggle with situations that seem to have no immediate solutions. Two situations where supportive measures are often called for are the death of a loved one and going through a separation or a divorce.

10

Stress and Crisis

Stress and pressures are a part of daily life. Each person we counsel has his or her own set of stresses and pressures, such as handling a rebellious teenage daughter, coping with an unreasonable boss or facing the prospect of major surgery. The way people deal with stress varies from one person to the next. One person freely discusses a personal concern with a friend, comes to a decision as to what should be done and then does what needs to be done; another reacts to the stressful situation by increased smoking, overeating or drinking too much, a third is overwhelmed and unable to function any longer. Why one person can handle a stressful situation decisively and with equanimity and another is incapacitated by it is linked to the way the person looks at the stressful situation, early training, and learned coping methods.

Most of us usually can handle ordinary stresses on our own but we find that talking with another helps to lessen our tension and sometimes gives us a different perspective. When we discuss something with another we often are able to see the matter from a different point of view and as a consequence take steps which we had not previously considered. Many people who come for pastoral counseling could probably resolve whatever is bothering them without help but they seek assistance because they find talking to a pastoral counselor helps them resolve their problem more easily. Also they feel that you as pastoral counselor will be able to help them see how their Christian faith relates to the stressful situation and show them how to use this faith in finding a solution to their problem.

When some people are faced with a persistent stressful situation and unable to find any way out, they try one solution, then another and then still another; with each failure, their level of anxiety increases until they find themselves in a state of crisis. "A crisis is a temporary state of upset and disorganization, characterized chiefly by an individual's inability to cope with a particular situation using customary methods of problem solving."[1] It is usually precipitated by a threat to survival, bodily integrity, or some psychosocially determined need perceived to have a life or death value. What is lost or threatened to be lost is so important to the individual that he or she feels unable to live without it.[2]

AN EXAMPLE OF A CRISIS

The following is an example of a person in a state of crisis which illustrates the various components found in most crises.

Mrs. Jones is the mother of three daughters, aged ten, fourteen, and seventeen. She works as a secretary; her husband is a machinist. Two months ago her husband lost his job. He made every effort to find another but with no success. As a consequence, he became depressed and gave up looking for work. Lately he has been drinking excessively and become abusive with both Mrs. Jones and their daughters.

A month ago, the oldest daughter fainted at school and later was diagnosed as being diabetic, which greatly upset Mrs. Jones. In some way, Mrs. Jones felt she was responsible because she chose to work when the children were small. Had she not worked, she thought that she could have spent more time with her children and then might have detected signs of the diabetes long before this.

Six months ago Mrs. Jones was in an automobile accident in which her car was severely damaged and she received a neck injury. Since she did not notice a stop signal, ran through it and hit an on-coming car, she was responsible for the accident. Ostensibly Mrs. Jones came to the counselor in pastoral ministry because she wanted help in dealing with her husband's drinking. As she talked, it became clear that what she really wanted was to talk about herself. Recently she had found it difficult to concentrate at work; she seemed tense and anxious most of the time. She found herself crying for no apparent reason, which was particularly upsetting to her because she seldom cried before and was afraid that she would lose her job and then the family would have no means of support.

COMPONENTS OF THE CRISIS

So as to understand more clearly the nature of a crisis, let us consider some of its elements as demonstrated in this example. First of all, we note a change in Mrs. Jones' mental state and behavior. Previous to the crisis reaction, she was an efficient secretary, a good wife and mother and a pleasant person to be around; now she is unable to meet the demands of work and home and no longer the person she used to be. Secondly, we see that three events that threatened her sense of well-being took place over the course of six months, any one of which she probably could have handled without going into a state of crisis since she is basically a strong person. It was a combination of three stressful events that overwhelmed her, which is often the case in many crises.[3] It should also be noted that it is not necessarily the event that causes the crisis reaction but what this event means to the individual, which partially explains why an event or series of events become a crisis for one person but not for another. In all three events Mrs. Jones considered herself a failure. She thought that she had not been sufficiently understanding and compassionate with her husband and thus had caused him to become depressed and resort to excessive drinking. She also thought that she was responsible, at least to some extent, for her daughter's diabetic condition because she considered herself neglectful when her daughter was a small child. And, finally, she blamed herself for the automobile accident which had put a strain on the family finances. People who are in the midst of a crisis are given to self-recrimination and depleted self-esteem. They frequently blame themselves for happenings over which they have little or no control.

Each of the three above-mentioned events placed demands on Mrs. Jones' coping skills. She tried to be compassionate with her husband when he lost his job but it was not enough to keep him from slipping into a depression and drinking excessively. None of her children had ever been seriously sick before, so she had no experience to fall back on when faced with the serious illness of her daughter. And, finally, she blamed herself for the accident and the financial strain it put on the family. She tried to talk about the accident with her husband but he was unsympathetic and overly concerned about the cost to repair the car and her medical bills. In every crisis one of the main causes for the reaction is a breakdown in coping skills. Once the usual coping skills are no longer effective, the person has nowhere to turn, tries to solve the problem in a hit and miss manner, which usually fails, and ends up feeling that the whole situation is hopeless.

FAILURE TO COPE

As we grow up, we learn ways of handling the demands and problems of everyday life. When the occasion calls for it, we automatically make use of these learned ways of coping. However, we run into difficulties when we are forced to face new situations for which we have no coping skills or the skills we have learned prove ineffective.

"The usual coping skills are not always adequate for a given problem for a variety of reasons: 1) A problem may be just too great and overwhelming—death of a family member, for example. 2) A problem may have some significance that makes it overwhelming. One man may adjust relatively easily to the loss of a limb, while the same loss may represent overwhelming stress for another man, perhaps because of his occupation or because of some interpersonal meaning. 3) A problem might occur at a time of special vulnerability—I might ordinarily handle a flooded basement with relative equanimity, but if it occurs while I have the flu, it might seem like a catastrophe. A series of problems within a short time may deplete a person's ability to cope. 4) A problem may come when a person's usual coping mechanisms are blocked—my wife may have just left me, and so I cannot discuss a new problem with her as I usually do. 5) A problem may occur for which the person is unprepared because it is new to him and he has never developed applicable coping mechanisms. For example, if I handle all my family problems by taking charge and giving orders, the blossoming adolescence of my first child may eventually leave me feeling helpless."[5]

INDIVIDUALIZED REACTION TO STRESS

People differ in their reaction to stressful situations. What constitutes a crisis for one becomes a challenge for another.

Whether the situation provokes a crisis reaction depends upon a number of factors. First, and perhaps the most important, is the meaning of the event to the individual.[6] Any event that is looked upon as seriously threatening to physical or psychological survival makes that event potentially crisis-provoking. For instance, Mrs. Jones in the case cited above looked upon financial solvency as a matter of life and death. Her husband's loss of a job, her daughter's medical bills and the cost of her accident all presented a major threat to her sense of financial security. Another person may have taken the same events more philosophically and figured that she would get by with unemployment insurance and a little help from relatives.

One's self-image and level of self-confidence have a direct bearing on whether an event or series of events cause a crisis reaction or not. If a person has a poor opinion of himself or herself and limited self-confidence, events ordinarily taken in stride by others become threatening and crisis-provoking. Mrs. Jones, for example, had a relatively poor opinion of herself. She tended to blame herself for any misfortune that occurred. Repeated use of this tendency gradually diminished her self-esteem and contributed to her crisis reaction.

Past experience can determine how we view a situation and how we adjust to it in the future. For instance, if we have been raised in an affluent home and led to believe that keeping this life-style is most important, any serious threat to this life-style can provoke, at least partially, the crisis reaction.

LOSS AS PRECIPITATING THE CRISIS

The loss of something we consider most important can precipitate a crisis. Typical examples of a loss are the death of a parent, divorce, the loss of a job or retirement. Sometimes anticipating a loss can be just as crisis-provoking as an actual loss. Some graduating seniors find themselves in a state of crisis as they anticipate losing the protected environment of a university campus and go out into the competitive world of business. Strange as it may appear, a promotion at work can also bring on the same reaction in a man who questions his ability to handle the responsibilities of a new job. What the loss means to the individual often determines whether he or she will surmount it or lapse into a state of crisis.

The violation of one's ideals can bring about a loss of self-esteem and the esteem of others. Incarceration for driving under the influence of alcohol or being arrested for possession of narcotics can result in a crisis, depending upon how much damage these episodes do to the person's self-esteem. And, finally, any sudden change in status that damages physical and psychological well-being and involves a loss in some way can bring on a crisis reaction, such as a serious injury in an automobile accident, radical surgery or contracting an incurable disease.

RECOGNIZING THE SIGNS OF A CRISIS

Recognizing that a person is in a state of crisis is not always easy. People react differently: for some the signs are clear; for others there are almost no signs. Any radical change in behavior is probably the most significant indicator of a crisis reaction. The outgoing, lively person suddenly becomes quiet and withdrawn; the usually tranquil person becomes volatile and agitated. Some people are given to crying spells for no apparent reason, which has never happened before. And, finally, some show obvious signs of depression, such as sadness, tiredness, self-deprecation and changes in patterns of eating and sleeping.

The most difficult people to counsel are those who "stonewall" the way they feel. They appear to be handling quite well the loss of their job or the break-up of a long-time marriage. They take the hurt philosophically and say, "Everything happens for a purpose. I may not be able to see the reason now, but someday I hope to." Or they cover over their true feelings by relying on their faith: "It's God's will. God must have a better job in store for me." They deny their true feelings of anger or resentment by spiritualizing them and fail to acknowledge how they really feel about the loss. Later when they find themselves in a similar situation, their true feelings may surface and can escalate the new crisis reaction.

ANXIETY AND DEPRESSION

Anxiety and depression are the two most common feelings experienced by people in the state of crisis, with one or both being present.[7] Anxiety manifests itself in a variety of ways and can affect almost every organ in the body. Anxiety makes the person feel overwhelmed by a sense of fear, dread, and apprehension. You may hear the person say: "I feel so nervous and scared, as though something terrible is going to happen." Rapid heartbeat, pains in the chest, inappropriate perspiration and a general sense of restlessness may all be signs of anxiety, as well as complaints about impaired concentration or an inability to think clearly and make decisions. Other signs of anxiety are feeling edgy, being irritable and being impulsive.

Depression is another common feeling found in people who are in a state of crisis. Occasionally we all feel down and blue, but this feeling is very different from depression. Depression is marked by feelings of dejection, sadness, despair and worthlessness. Depressed people are pessimistic, think negatively and show little interest in others or in what is happening in the world outside of themselves. They also experience guilt and anger. Often the anger is directed at themselves, blaming themselves for being in the depression. These depressed people need to ventilate their feelings and then link these feelings to what is causing them.

HELPING PEOPLE IN CRISIS

What can be done to help people in the state of crisis?

First of all, you can help them talk about the crisis situation with all its anxiety, pain, fear and depression. You can be empathetic to expressions of sadness, rejection, and helplessness. You can allow them to cry or express their anger, even at God, without their fearing that you will condemn them. You can help them face the situation that provoked the crisis in manageable doses. At times their emotional distress may seem overwhelming and you may want to distract them for a while and then at the appropriate time lead them back to what is so disturbing. You can offer hope without giving false assurances. You can help them get a clearer picture of the facts. Sometimes people in the state of crisis are confused and fail to see the world as it actually is. If they blame others for their misfortune, you can try to get them to focus on themselves and their crisis situation because blaming others is just another way of avoiding reality.

You can help them find possible ways of handling the crisis situation and then settle on the solution that seems most likely to succeed. If there are several problems, you can help them focus on one at a time. If we allow people to tackle all of their problems at once, they are liable to find answers to none. And, finally, you can assist them in implementing what they have decided to do about the problem.

BEING SUPPORTIVE

Many people in crisis simply need the support of another person until they can regain their equilibrium. An attentive, interested listener can give them this support. Your first and perhaps most important task is to listen attentively to what the person has to say. Listening calls for focusing our full attention on the counselee, hearing what is said, what is hinted at but never said, the tone used, the expression employed, and even what is never mentioned. Pointing out the counselee's strengths and downplaying his or her weaknesses is being supportive. You can also listen to your own thoughts and feelings to see if they are going to get in the way of your helping this person.

Most people who come for pastoral counseling know why they have come and they know what they want to get out of it. With a minimum of prompting they will give their story. It is essential for you as pastoral counselor to listen attentively, understand what has happened and how the counselee feels about what has happened. It also helps to know why the person came today rather than two weeks or a month ago because people generally react to a crisis shortly after the event that precipitated it, which can help to pinpoint the reason for the crisis reaction.

Due to emotional turmoil many counselees in crisis are confused and often cannot tell you what took place prior to the onset of the crisis reaction. When this happens, your first task as counselors is to help these counselees become aware of how they feel and the reasons why they feel the way they do.[8] After expressing their feelings they usually can begin to use their cognitive faculties once again. Their memories become sharper and they begin to think more clearly.

"Cognitive restoration is needed because the emotional

state resulting from the precipitating event is so painful that the client's goal is to avoid or defend against the painful effect, not resolve the crisis. The premise of cognitive restoration is the belief that knowledge and understanding, after a thorough ventilation of feelings, reduce emotional overloading, restore cognitive functioning, and facilitate regaining cognitive control. In other words, by providing an explanation to the client of the reason for the crisis reaction and the meaning of his or her behavior, the therapist helps the client regain mastery over his or her life."[9]

ESTABLISHING RAPPORT

In any kind of counseling, good rapport is most important. In crisis counseling, it is essential because most people in the state of crisis feel that their situation is hopeless and that they are helpless to do anything about it. It is only when they place their hope in a counselor to help them that these feelings of hopelessness and helplessness begin to subside and they can then start to help themselves with your assistance. To develop rapport you need to show genuine concern for the person in crisis and an understanding of what that person is experiencing. Moreover, you need to be relaxed and friendly, exhibit self-confidence, and reassure the person that the problem provoking the crisis can be resolved if he or she and you work together.

At the time of a crisis some people think they are losing their minds. It is often a relief for them to find out that what they are experiencing is the same as others have experienced when they found themselves in a similar situation. Gaining control over their fear of going insane helps these counselees to reestablish emotional equilibrium.

SUMMARIZING WHAT THE
COUNSELEE HAS SAID

After listening attentively to what the counselee has said, it often helps if you summarize what you have heard. This summary should contain the core of the problem and how the counselee feels about it.[10] Summarizing forces you to put into words the gist of the counselee's problem as you see it and allows the counselee to correct any misunderstandings. It tells the person that you have been listening and understand what the problem is. Often summarizing prompts the counselee to add details that have been overlooked.

After you have heard the counselee's account of what took place, you may want more information so as to clarify parts of the account that you do not understand. For instance, you may want to know how a man feels about his wife and whether he has any close friends since he only vaguely alluded to how he gets along with his wife and others. The purpose of this information is to help you assist the counselee later on when the two of you are searching for a workable solution.

LOOKING FOR POSSIBLE SOLUTIONS

Once you feel that you have an adequate understanding of the counselee's situation, it is usually helpful to inquire whether the person has ever been in a similar predicament, what he or she did, and whether this solved the problem. What the person did in the past may help him or her to find a workable solution for the present situation. For example, a middle-aged woman tells you that she lost a son in an automobile accident three months ago and has been paralyzed with depression ever since. When you ask her if she has ever experienced a death in her family before, she tells you that when her mother died several years ago she coped with her death by forcing herself to visit relatives and friends, even though she did not feel like doing this. Taking the same measures may be the best solution in her present circumstances. If the counselee has not been in a similar situation or has tried the same coping method but to no avail, then the next step is to help the counselee search for other possible ways of handling the problem as was described in the process of problem-solving.

In looking for alternative ways, you may take any of three approaches depending upon the emotional state of the counselee: (1) be non-directive, (2) collaborate with the counselee, or (3) be directive.

In the non-directive approach, the counselor has the person suggest possible ways of solving the crisis-problem and then has him or her evaluate what favors and what is against each of the options. In this approach you as counselor act as a sounding board and set up a structured method which helps the counselee discover a way to cope with his or her problem. When counselees are intelligent and verbal and the crisis reaction is not severe, this approach is usually effective.

The cooperative approach is the one most commonly used. Here you and the counselee work together at searching for possible ways to solve the problem that caused the crisis. Sometimes you may have to suggest options the counselee overlooked, but the choice of the option that looks most likely to succeed is left to the counselee.

And, finally, sometimes counselees are so confused and emotionally upset that they are unable to see any way out of their crisis situation. In this case, your best approach is to be direct and tell these individuals what you think they should do. These people usually feel that their situation is hopeless and that no one can help them. Your advice, especially if it seems reasonable to the counselee, can give the counselee a glimmer of hope and he or she may leave the counseling session determined to try what you have suggested.

The fact that people in crisis have decided what they must do to get out of the state of crisis does not mean that they will implement their decision. Usually these people need to settle on what steps they must take. An essential part of crisis counseling is to help the person formulate a series of concrete steps he or she can take to implement the previously made decision. These steps should be specific, such as getting a depressed woman to decide when she will telephone a friend to arrange for a visit since people in the state of crisis frequently have trouble organizing their activities and following through on what they have decided unless you exert some pressure on them.

Follow-up sessions may be needed to encourage the counselee to keep working toward a solution to his or her problem. If the plan decided upon in the previous session failed to resolve the crisis, then a new strategy can be devised or an option that was rejected can be reconsidered.

SUMMARY

A crisis is characterized by a debilitating emotional reaction to an event or series of events seen or anticipated as threatening to the individual's physical and/or psychological well-being and security and an inability to cope with this threat by the use of one's usual coping strategies. It is frequently connected with some kind of a loss, such as the loss of a spouse through death or divorce or the loss of employment.

Some indicators of a crisis are (1) radical change in the way a person acts, (2) overreacting or underreacting emotionally, (3) withdrawal from usual social life, and (4) mental confusion and indecision.

Intervention consists of clearly defining the problem that caused the crisis, emotional ventilation, reestablishing cognitive mastery and helping the individual resolve the crisis through a problem-solving technique.

11

Making Referrals

Most people who seek your help come with problems you can handle. Occasionally, however, you will encounter people whose problems are so complex, whose way of thinking so distorted, or whose behavior is so bizarre that they call for help beyond the scope of your expertise. Usually these individuals need to be referred to a psychiatrist or psychologist.

At times you may find it difficult deciding whom to counsel and whom to refer. The obviously psychotic or the seriously neurotic person presents little difficulty; the decision to refer is relatively simple. People who are somewhat neurotic and whose problems are connected with their neurosis can be perplexing. You have to make an evaluation and then decide whether to undertake the counseling yourself or refer the person to someone better qualified.

With experience most counselors in pastoral ministry discover the extent of their expertise. They become proficient in determining whom they can help and whom they cannot and should refer to a psychiatrist or psychologist. In addition to mental illness, there are a number of other circumstances that call for a referral. First and perhaps the most important is the amount of time you have available for counseling. Usually those engaged in pastoral counseling have other obligations and responsibilities. Counseling is only one of their many functions. They cannot afford to counsel a large number of people whom they see once or even twice a week over an extended period of time. In general, it can be said that most counseling in pastoral ministry should probably be limited to one or two sessions. However, some counselors in pastoral ministry have three or four people whom they see on a regular basis but usually find that additional counselees interfere with their other responsibilities. Consequently, they often refer to a psychologist or marriage counselor others who seek counseling and appear to need more than a couple of sessions.

As a rule people who are seriously disturbed or have complex personality problems make slow progress. Moreover, they need to be seen weekly or even more frequently. Counselors who spend their time and energy on a few individuals cannot do justice to all the other people who seek their help and to their other responsibilities.

The cost of treatment can be another factor in deciding whether to make a referral. Counseling and psychotherapy are expensive and many people cannot afford it. However, you should not allow this obstacle to arouse your sympathy and agree to counsel someone you know you should not. Frequently these needy people can find counseling centers where the fees are set on their ability to pay. Knowing about these centers and the conditions under which they admit new clients can help you resist the temptation to accept someone whom you realize you should not counsel for any of a number of reasons.

WHO SHOULD BE REFERRED?

The most obvious person to refer is the person who manifests clear signs of abnormal thinking, feeling, and acting.

These signs may take the form of hallucinations or delusions, such as the woman who says she sees and talks with Jesus regularly because she is the fourth person of the Trinity or the man who is convinced that the local bishop can read his mind and is stealing his ideas on how to make money. Or they may take the form of a serious depression with suicidal ruminations. If you ask, you are likely to discover that many of these people have a long history of visiting psychiatrists and psychologists. Any suggestion that they seek psychiatric help often meets with opposition because psychotic people are usually convinced that their thoughts and beliefs are true, and therefore they do not need psychiatric help. In most of these cases, the best assistance you can give is not to "buy into" their psychotic thinking and keep insisting that they need help beyond your capability. To argue with them about the lack of validity to their delusions may strengthen these delusions.

PARANOID PERSONALITY DISORDER

Personality is "a complex pattern of deeply embedded psychological characteristics that express themselves automatically in almost every facet of functioning . . . and comprise the individual's distinctive pattern of perceiving, feeling, thinking and coping. When personality traits are characterized by an inflexible and maladaptive response to stress, and cause significant disability in working and relating to others, then a personality disorder exists."[1] One such personality disorder is the paranoid person. The essential feature of this disorder is a "permanent and unshakable delusional system accompanied by the preservation of clear and orderly thinking."[2] Usually the paranoid's delusions are clearly stated and may sound quite valid when you first hear them but actually they are erroneous. An example of paranoid thinking might be the businessman who accuses his wife of having an affair with another man and trying to undermine his health by leaving the windows open, when actually his wife has always been faithful and solicitous about his health. No matter how much his wife and others who speak for her attest to her fidelity and solicitude for him, he clings doggedly to his convictions. People who have a paranoid personality disorder almost always need psychiatric help. They are beyond your expertise. Usually they think that they do not need this help because they are convinced that what they think is valid. You should expect that they will reject your suggestion to seek professional help. Sometimes it is helpful to refer the paranoid to his or her family doctor and then let the doctor make the referral. In this case, either you or a relative should warn the doctor about the delusional system before the paranoid sees the doctor.

NEUROSIS

Probably the most common personality disorder encountered in pastoral ministry is some form of a neurosis. Neurotic disorders include: (1) persistent and irrational fears of a specific object, activity or situation, such as the fear of going into a large church building or the fear of meeting people other than those in their immediate family; (2) obsessions and compulsions, such as washing their hands in a ritualistic fashion many times during a single day or severe scrupulosity; (3) persistent complaints of failing health with little or no validity for their complaints.[3] Often these latter people say they have consulted many doctors and have received no relief, so now they are turning to God and prayer. People whose neurotic condition is not severe can sometimes be helped by an empathetic counselor. Most, however, need most intensive and prolonged care and thus should be referred to a psychiatrist or clinical psychologist.

DEPRESSION

Depression is one of the most common disorders in our times, especially among the middle aged and elderly. Some characteristics of depression are (1) sadness, (2) feeling that one's life is empty and meaningless, (3) feeling helpless and without hope of recovery, (4) suicidal ruminations, (5) the disruption of normal sleeping and eating patterns, (6) feeling worthless, and (7) failing to care for one's appearance and personal hygiene.[4] Pastoral counseling and advice usually have little or no impact on a depression, which often lasts for a year or two and is too deep-seated and complex to respond to the ordinary procedures of pastoral counseling. A severe depression calls for medication and a special type of psychotherapy with a psychiatrist or a psychologist working in conjunction with a psychiatrist. In the case of a moderate depression, however, psychotherapy alone may be sufficient. It is the task of the counselor in pastoral ministry to detect the presence of a depression and then make a referral. Often a depression weakens the depressed person's faith and sometimes kills all desire to pray. To suggest greater fidelity to prayer and the sacraments as a remedy is meaningless or can cause the person to feel even more guilty because he or she is unable to put your advice into practice. You should keep in mind that it is not unusual for the depressed person to feel abandoned by God or even to question the existence of God.

ALCOHOL AND DRUG ABUSE

Counselors in pastoral ministry sometimes encounter alcoholics or those who abuse drugs; more often, however, it is the relative of the abuser who comes for counseling because he or she wants to help the abuser but does not know what to do.

In general, alcoholics and addicts derive little benefit from pastoral counseling because their mental processes are too debilitated by the chemical substances in their systems. It is possible to spend an hour talking with an alcoholic and he or she will not remember talking with you, let alone what you said.[5] The alcoholic and drug abuser needs to be withdrawn from the destructive substance in a gradual and systematic way and then complete a program of rehabilitation, a part of which often includes psychological and spiritual counseling. In most communities there are centers for the treatment of alcoholics and drug addicts. The best help you can give these individuals is to make a successful referral to a local alcohol and drug abuse rehabilitation center and then be available when the person returns from the center. In many cities throughout the United States there are priests, sisters and lay people who are knowledgeable in the treatment of alcoholics and drug abusers and make this field their principal ministry. They can be excellent resources in helping you make a good referral.

ANTISOCIAL PERSONALITY DISORDER

Sometimes counselors in pastoral ministry encounter people whose behavior is immature and grossly irresponsible. Psychologists classify many of these adults as antisocial personalities. The individual with an antisocial personality disorder manifests a number of the following characteristics: (1) an inability to keep a job, usually because of absenteeism, irresponsibility and limited ability to relate with employers and fellow employees; (2) a lack of an ability to function as a parent, as manifested by physical and psychological neglect of their children; (3) a lack of respect for law, as evidenced by criminal and illegal activity; (4) an inability to maintain a lasting sex relationship, as evidenced by repeated marriages or relationships outside of marriage; (5) failure to honor financial obligations; (6) failure to plan ahead and acting impulsively.[6]

If the person is a teenager, the following are indicative of an antisocial personality: (1) running away from home several times; (2) truancy; (3) chronic violation of rules at home and at school; (4) school grades markedly below expectations; (5) persistent lying; (6) criminal activity, such as theft and vandalism.[7]

If the adult or teenager with whom you are speaking manifests several of the behavior characteristics listed above, you can suspect that this person has an antisocial personality and is in need of assistance beyond your capability. They need not manifest all of the characteristics noted above to be diagnosed as having an antisocial personality disorder. These individuals usually have a winning personality and appear to be quite normal on your first meeting them. However, they are most adept at manipulating others to their own advantage. Treatment is most difficult because antisocial people can see no reason for their being in treatment. They are content to remain as they are since they experience little or no guilt, even when they perpetrate outrageous wrongs and bring great suffering into the lives of others. They are often unable to relate to others in a meaningful way, aside from using others to further their own ends. Lying is a way of life because truth is anything that helps to promote themselves. The best assistance you can give to the person with an antisocial personality disorder is not to let them manipulate you and recommend professional help, even though the antisocial person will usually reject your suggestion. By recommending professional help, you are telling the person that you think he or she has a psychological problem, which usually that person is unwilling to admit.

Anyone who has worked in a parish rectory for any length of time quickly discovers that a large percentage of people who come for help are really coming to get a "handout." A number of these people fall under the category of an antisocial personality disorder. They tell you a fabricated story about being able to get a job in another town if they only had the bus fare, and then ask you for money. They usually are very personable and readily change the story to fit the situation and the personality of the counselor. They know that there is not an element of truth in their story but truth for them is what is going to get the money. To give such persons what they want—and there are many more men with this disorder than women—simply strengthens their pattern of behavior. Of course, everyone who asks for money is not suffering from an antisocial personality disorder. Often people in real need come for help. Your task is to distinguish between the two and then treat each in a way that will help them.

SUICIDAL PEOPLE

Occasionally counselors in pastoral ministry are called upon to help people who are thinking of ending their own lives. In this case, it is extremely important that counselors try to determine as soon as possible whom they should attempt to help and whom they should refer to a psychiatrist or psychologist. Research has shown that some suicidal people present a greater risk of ending their own lives than others. People who are high risks are (1) those who have a detailed plan of what they will do to kill themselves, such as a plan to take fifty sleeping pills they have hidden in their bathroom closet or to get their brother's gun in the nightstand next to his bed and go down into his basement and shoot themselves; (2) the elderly who are in poor health or have a terminal disease; (3) people who have a history of instability, moving from one place to another, from one job to another and relying excessively on alcohol or drugs; (4) people who have attempted to commit suicide before; (5) people who live alone and are cut off from almost all social contacts.[8] The detailed plan and previous attempts are the most important single indicators of a high risk person.[9] Some other facts that should be taken into consideration are: (1) two-thirds of the men and one-half of the women who have committed suicide are over the age of forty-five; (2) the risk of successful suicide is higher among men but women make more attempts; (3) divorced and separated people, especially if they live alone, have a high rate of suicide; (4) severely depressed people, especially when the depression is beginning to lessen, are high risks; (5) Catholics have a lower rate of suicide than other religious groups or non-believers; (6) people who have been hospitalized within the last six months are high risk.[10]

In dealing with the potentially suicidal person, the first task of the counselor is to determine how high a risk the person is, which means that the counselor will have to ask the person whether he or she has been thinking of committing suicide and how seriously. Some counselors mistakenly think that they will put the thought of committing suicide into the person's mind if they bring up the topic, whereas the truth is that most people are relieved if you ask them whether they have thought of ending their lives. If they have had no suicidal thoughts, they will tell you; if they have been thinking of suicide, they appreciate your mentioning suicide and will probably want to talk about it. If they have had suicidal ruminations, the levels of risk indicated above should be considered and weighed. If the person appears to be a high risk, then he or she should be referred to a psychiatrist who can hospitalize the person, if this is necessary. You should, therefore, have in mind the name of a psychiatrist, call him or her, and arrange for the appointment. It is essential that you get the person in contact with the psychiatrist as quickly as possible, lest the person commit suicide in the interval. If the person is a low risk, that is, he or she has thought of suicide but not seriously, has no plan, and has never attempted suicide before, then you can probably handle the matter yourself.

People who are thinking of suicide are ambivalent; they want to take their own lives and they don't. In counseling such people, you should focus on the reasons why they don't want to take their own lives, such as the effect their death will have on their children or parents. It is best to get the person to suggest the reasons against committing suicide rather than for you to suggest them, lest what you suggest only increase their feeling guilty. These reasons should be fully discussed along with the possibility of the person actually taking his or her own life.

There are numerous other forms of mental and emotional disorders besides those described above. Most counselors in pastoral ministry will find it worthwhile to study the Diagnostic and Statistical Manual of Mental Disorders (DSM-III) published by the American Psychiatric Association and also to read some recently published articles on mental disorders so as to recognize the various personality disorders when they see them in their counselees.

TO WHOM SHOULD YOU MAKE A REFERRAL?

Once you have made the decision to refer a counselee, the next question is "To whom?" Often mental illness has a physical as well as a psychological basis, which is especially true in cases of severe mental illnesses.[11] Consequently, those who are severely disturbed generally should be referred to a psychiatrist, who is a medical doctor and can prescribe medication as well as offer psychotherapy. The psychiatrist's skill in handling both chemical therapy and psychotherapy is a good measure of his or her competence. An important part of a psychiatrist's practice is diagnosis and the choice of the most suitable therapy for the particular person. Therefore, when the

individual seems to you to be quite disturbed and you are uncertain as to the diagnosis, he or she should be referred to a
psychiatrist.

There are, however, some mental and emotional distur-
bances which other professionals are well equipped to handle.
One of these professionals is the clinical psychologist who is
trained to counsel people and offer psychotherapy. However,
clinical psychologists cannot prescribe medication because
they do not have a medical degree. Clinical psychologists usually have a doctorate in a clinical area of psychology and have
been licensed by the state where they work. Their training
consists of an intensive academic program over a period of four
or five years and an internship in a hospital or agency. Many
psychologists also take an added year or two of post-doctoral
work. In general, clinical psychologists are equipped to help
people with neurotic and adjustment problems. Some experienced psychologists care for psychotics but usually in conjunction with a psychiatrist who prescribes the proper
medication.

Marriage and family counselors are another source for referrals. Marriage and family counselors usually have a master's
degree in marriage and family counseling or counseling psychology and at least a year of supervised experience. In many
states, marriage and family counselors need certification before
they can practice. They are trained to handle marriage counseling and problems related to family life. However, some of
these counselors after several years of experience are able to
counsel people with serious personal problems and even engage in some kinds of psychotherapy. Since marriage and family counselors usually charge lower fees than psychiatrists or
psychologists, making a referral to a marriage and family counselor is more practical for people with limited finances and
whose personality disorder is minor.

In general, psychiatrists treat the more severe cases of

mental and emotional disorder, and psychologists and marriage and family counselors, the less severe. Therefore people who seek your help and show signs of a psychosis should be referred to a psychiatrist. Severely neurotic people can do well with either a psychiatrist or a clinical psychologist, depending upon the nature of the neurotic condition. The competence of the therapist should be the deciding factor. Problems in personal, social and vocational adjustment are the special concern of counseling psychologists; marriage counseling and family problems are the special concern of marriage and family counselors, but many psychologists also engage in marriage counseling and family problems. If you refer the person to a mental health clinic, the type of therapy and the choice of therapist is left to the judgment of the staff at the clinic. As a consequence, you do not have to decide on the most suitable type of help for the individual you are referring.

FAITH AND PSYCHOTHERAPY

One of the problems that confronts counselors in pastoral ministry when they need to make a referral is whether or not to send the person to a professional who holds the same religious convictions as that person. For instance, should a Catholic be referred to a Catholic psychiatrist, psychologist or marriage counselor? Is it wise to send a Catholic to a non-believing professional? Because of the relationship between psychiatry, psychology and religion, many people fear that their faith will be undermined by a non-believer. They often see psychotherapy as a process wherein the therapist gives advice which the patient should follow. They fear that the psychiatrist or psychologist will give them advice which is contrary to their faith. Unfortunately, people sometimes hear of instances where a psychotherapist has given such advice and tampered with a patient's religious convictions, but this does not mean that such tampering is a common practice among psychiatrists and psychologists.

In making a referral, both the psychotherapist's attitude toward religion and his or her competence must be taken into consideration. Professionals, just like the general population, have different attitudes toward religion and the church. Some are very much involved in their church and give a considerable amount of their time ministering to the members of the church, serving on committees, giving lectures, etc.; others believe what their church teaches but do not participate in it, or participate as little as possible; others believe in Christianity but see no value in belonging to a church and may even be opposed to all organized religions; still others are hostile to the very notion of religion and see religion as a crutch and indicative of a neurosis, which is the position of Sigmund Freud, who considered religion the opium of the people. Because of Freud's position and scientific methodology, more psychiatrists and psychologists seem to have a greater bias toward religion and the church than one would expect in the general population.

In counseling and psychotherapy a process called the "therapeutic alliance" usually takes place, which means that the patient or client comes to trust and respect the therapist and his or her views. Even though many therapists do not like to admit it, people tend to see their therapist as an authority who can bring about a cure if they cooperate with what he or she says. If psychotherapists allow a biased attitude toward religion to enter into their psychotherapy, they violate the therapeutic alliance, take undue advantage of the therapeutic relationship, and can influence adversely the patient's view of religion. Unfortunately, this occasionally has happened and some people have given up their faith as a result. An example of this can be found in Dr. M. Scott Peck's best seller *The Road Less Traveled*[12] where he reports the case of a young woman who gave up her Catholic faith as a result of the therapeutic alliance and the author's position on the Catholic Church. He contends that it was necessary for his patient to give up her faith in order to get better, a contention which one can validly question from a psychological point of view.

Some irreligious psychiatrists and psychologists have openly entered the realm of religion and morals and as a result caused considerable spiritual and psychological damage to their patients. Unfortunately, there are poor psychiatrists and psychologists, just as there are poor surgeons and obstetricians. However, this does not mean that we should condemn all psychiatrists and psychologists who have no religious convictions; instead we should investigate the attitude and competence of the professionals to whom we make a referral and how they deal with religious and moral issues when they arise in psychotherapy and counseling.

THE PROFESSIONAL'S ATTITUDE ON RELIGION

How do you know what a psychiatrist or psychologist holds and follows in regard to religious belief? Of course, the best way to know a professional is to be his or her friend, or at least to have had the opportunity to converse with him or her at some length about religious issues. Another way to know where professionals stand is to find out about their involvement in their church. If professionals give a portion of their time to worship and church activities, you can be relatively sure that they value their religious belief. Another way is to ask someone who has seen the professional about the professional's religious convictions. Frequently, however, you will find that people do not know what their psychiatrist or psychologist holds in regard to religion. They do not know whether he or she is a Catholic, Protestant, or Jew or has no religious belief. This generally means that the therapists were successful in keeping religion out of the therapeutic process and, if they have any biases in regard to religion, they have been successful in not allowing them to enter into the psychotherapy. A final way is to find out how well the person who recommended the professional to you knows the professional and then make your judgment as to his or her suitability for the particular counselee you intend to refer. However, it can be said that there is no substitute for knowing the professional personally, which means that you would do well to meet with a couple of psychiatrists, psychologists, and marriage and family counselors in your locale and discuss religious and other issues with them.

The second quality you need to look for is competence. Competent professionals are those who know their field, have had some experience, and have been at least relatively successful. We generally learn about the competence of the professionals through their colleagues or physicians who have referred a number of patients to the professional for treatment. Thus you need to know how reliable is the judgment of the colleague or physician who is making the recommendation. Another source of information is a former patient or client who can tell you whether he or she was satisfied or not with the professional's performance. If you know other psychiatrists and psychologists, often their judgment about the competence of the professional to whom you are thinking of referring someone can be helpful.

Basically, the problem of whether to refer a person to a psychiatrist, psychologist or marriage counselor of the same belief as the person being referred is resolved by your knowledge of the professional's attitude toward religion and the professional's reputation as a person of competence and integrity. If the psychotherapist with no religious affiliation has proven himself or herself to be competent and accepting of religion, there is little danger of his or her undermining the faith and morals of the person you want to refer. If investigation reveals that a professional has tampered with the religious and moral convictions of patients or clients, then that professional does not merit a referral. On the other hand, it is better to refer a person to a competent psychiatrist or psychologist with no religious convictions but an adequate understanding of and tolerance for what Christians believe than to a professional with firm religious convictions but lacking in competence.

MAKING A SUCCESSFUL REFERRAL

Success or failure in psychotherapy often depends upon the attitude of the patient. This attitude is usually formed before the person enters the office of the psychiatrist or psychologist. A goal of the counselor in pastoral ministry should be to try to lessen any negative attitudes that might hinder progress in psychotherapy.

For many people the suggestion that they see a psychiatrist or clinical psychologist has but one meaning, that they are crazy, which is the usual reaction of those who are uninformed. Counselors in pastoral ministry frequently encounter this reaction when they try to make a referral. Usually this view must be corrected before the counselee will accept psychiatric or psychological help.

Psychiatry is a branch of medicine concerned with the mentally ill. Most people can accept the suggestion that they visit a physician when they have a persistent pain in the stomach. If you point out to them that visiting a psychiatrist or psychologist is like seeing a doctor, only instead of taking care of a pain in the stomach it is to rid oneself of a depression, anxiety or some other emotional disorder, this can make the suggestion that they see a psychiatrist or psychologist more acceptable.

Psychotherapy, one of the major tools used by psychiatrists and psychologists, is simply a more intensive form of counseling. Most people can accept the suggestion that they see another counselor better qualified to handle their personal problems than you are but when the words psychotherapy and psychiatric treatment are used they balk. Sometimes it can be helpful to tell them that counseling and psychotherapy are so closely linked that it is sometimes difficult to determine where one ends and the other begins.[13] The kinds and degrees of emotional illness are innumerable, like the kinds and degrees of physical illness.[14] One of the principal aims of treatment is to deal with an emotional disturbance before it becomes seriously debilitating. If you can give the person some of these ideas, you may be able to make him or her more accepting of psychiatric and psychological help.

Success or failure in convincing the individual to accept treatment frequently depends upon your attitude. If you have the mistaken idea that there is something degrading and humiliating about psychiatric care, you will probably convey this attitude to your counselees. On the other hand, if you have a clear idea of what psychiatrists and psychologists do and a positive attitude toward these professions, the battle is half won.

One of the prerequisites for successful psychotherapy is that the client wants therapy. Some people are aware of the seriousness of their disorder and willingly accept the suggestion that they get treatment; others who have less anxiety about the seriousness of their condition are apt to be less motivated for treatment. You should investigate the individual's desire for psychotherapy and strengthen it as much as possible. A few minutes devoted to encouraging the person to accept treatment can determine the success or failure of the treatment.

You should keep in mind, however, that there are some people who are emotionally disturbed but unable to profit from treatment. There are emotional illnesses as well as physical illnesses that cannot be cured or even further ameliorated. For some people, borderline functioning is the best that can be expected. Others may consider them odd or different, but if these people can manage to get by, there is little purpose in pressing for better adjustment. If the person has already undergone prolonged psychiatric treatment or reports treatment under several psychiatrists or psychologists, it is probable that another referral would be of little value. In this situation, your task is to care for the spiritual well-being of the person as best you can under the circumstances. Perhaps through interest and concern you can help this person maintain a minimum psychological balance.

DISPELLING FALSE IDEAS

In making referrals, you can also help counselees by giving them an idea of what takes place in psychotherapy. Frequently this may merely call for dispelling false ideas about psychotherapy. Some people have the erroneous notion that psychiatrists and psychologists tell clients what they must do to get better and that in a short time the disorder disappears if they do what they are told to do. Actually the person in therapy does most of the work and the therapist gives little advice. Under the direction of the therapist, individuals probe the depths of their personalities and thus come to a better understanding of themselves. They can then change their habitual ways of thinking, acting, and relating with others. The change, however, must come from within the person; the psychotherapist does not change the person.

During the initial sessions in therapy, most people are somewhat baffled by the inactivity of the psychiatrist or psychologist. This stage of initial confusion may be prevented somewhat if the counselees are forewarned that they must do the work themselves and that there are no pat answers that bring about a cure.

Pastoral counselors who become skilled in referring counselees for psychiatric or psychological treatment earn the gratitude of both the counselee and the psychotherapist. They do much to make the journey back to sound mental health easier and more comfortable.

After you have made a successful referral, your obligation to the counselee does not end. Counselees remain people of faith during the process of psychiatric and psychological treatment. They still need their relationship with God and the church. You, as a pastoral counselor, should try to help the individual in psychotherapy derive the greatest possible benefit from his or her religious commitment. This may mean occasional visits with you during the course of psychotherapy to strengthen the religious commitment. At this time questions and doubts about religion can be discussed as well as any conflicts between religion and psychiatry that may arise. The continuing relationship with you can have great significance to the former counselee and hasten the time when he or she no longer needs psychiatric or psychological care.

References

1. Introduction and Overview

1. Allen E. Ivey and J. Authier, *Microcounseling* (2nd ed.). Springfield, Ill.: Charles C. Thomas, 1978.

2. Robert R. Carkhuff, *Helping and Human Relations*, Vol. I: *Selection and Training*. New York: Holt, Rinehart & Winston, 1969, p. 4.

3. Robert R. Carkhuff and B. G. Berenson, *Beyond Counseling and Psychotherapy* (2nd ed.). New York: Holt, Rinehart & Winston, 1977.

4. Gerald Egan, *The Skilled Helper* (2nd ed). Monterey: Brooks/Cole, 1982, pp. 86–87.

5. Carkhuff, *op. cit.*, p. 174.

6. *Ibid.*, p. 175.

7. Egan, *op. cit.*, p. 127.

8. Carkhuff, *op. cit.*, pp. 185–186.

9. *Ibid.*, p. 184.

10. Carkhuff, *op. cit.*, p. 179.

11. Egan, *op. cit.*, pp. 120–121.

12. George M. Gazda, *Human Relations Development*. Boston: Allyn & Bacon, 1973, p. 87.

13. Allen E. Ivey, *Intentional Interviewing and Counseling*. Monterey: Brooks/Cole, 1983.

14. D.N. Dixon and J.A. Glover, *Counseling: A Problem Solving Approach*. New York: John Wiley & Sons, 1984.

2. Counseling in Pastoral Ministry

1. Gary S. Belkin, *Introduction to Counseling*. Dubuque: Wm. C. Brown, 1984, pp. 20–25.
2. William J. Connolly, "Contemporary Spiritual Direction: Scope and Principles." St. Louis: American Assistancy Seminar on Jesuit Spirituality, June 1975, pp. 102–103.
3. Eugene F. Bleidorn, *Help Me Father*. Milwaukee: Bruce, 1960, pp. 13–14.
4. Raymond Hostie, *Pastoral Counseling*. New York: Sheed and Ward, 1960, p. 10.
5. Lawrence M. Brammer, *The Helping Relationship* (3rd ed.). Englewood Cliffs: Prentice-Hall, 1985, p. 2.
6. Michael E. Cavanagh, *The Counseling Experience*. Monterey: Brooks/Cole, 1982, pp. 157–159.
7. Eric Berne, *Games People Play*. New York: Grove Press, 1964, p. 116.
8. Carl R. Rogers, *A Way of Being*. Boston: Houghton Mifflin, 1980, pp. 27–45.
9. *Ibid.*, p. 142.
10. David G. Martin, *Counseling and Therapy Skills*, Monterey: Brooks/Cole, 1983, pp. 3–16.
11. Carl R. Rogers, *Client Centered Therapy*. Boston: Houghton Mifflin, pp. 172–196.
12. Gerald Egan, *The Skilled Helper* (2nd ed.). Monterey: Brooks Cole, 1982, pp. 223–291.

3. Christian Faith and Values

1. Eugene Joly, *What Is Faith?* New York: Paulist Press, 1963, p. 111.
2. John L. Tracy, "Faith and Growth: A Psychology of Faith," in John P. Keating's *Faith in the Face of Doubt*. New York: Paulist Press, 1968, pp. 3–5.

3. Richard P. Vaughan, "Growth in Christian Faith," *Human Development*, 5, 3, 1984, p. 40.

4. B. Pascal, "The Work of the Pastoral Counselor," *Insight*, 11, 2, 1963, p. 5.

5. Antonio Royo and Jordan Aumann, *The Theology of Christian Perfection*. Dubuque: Priory Press, 1962, pp. 626–630.

6. Leland E. Hensie and Robert J. Campbell, *Psychiatric Dictionary*. New York: Oxford Press, 1976, p. 802.

7. Ernest G. Brier and David G. Young, *The Silent Language of Psychotherapy* (2nd ed.). New York: Aldine, 1984, p. 9.

8. Martha Perry and M.J. Furukawa, "Modeling Methods," in F.H. Kanfer and A. P. Goldstein, *Helping People Change* (2nd ed.). New York: Pergamon, 1980, p. 131.

9. *Ibid.*, p. 136.

10. *Ibid.*

11. *Ibid.*

12. S.M. Jourard, *The Transparent Self* (rev. ed.). New York: Van Nostrand Reinhold, 1971.

4. Feelings and Emotions

1. Gordon W. Allport, *Pattern and Growth in Personality*. New York: Holt, Rinehart and Winston, 1961, pp. 198–199.

2. Magda B. Arnold, *Emotion and Personality*. New York: Columbia University Press, 1960, pp. 74–75.

3. Rochelle S. Albin, *Emotions*. Philadelphia: The Westminister Press, 1983, p. 13.

4. *Ibid.*, p. 15.

5. Arnold, *op. cit.*, p. 194.

6. *Ibid.*, p. 210.

7. Donald O. Hebb, *A Textbook of Psychology*. Philadelphia: W. B. Saunders, 1966, p. 239.

8. Arnold, *op. cit.*, p. 258.

9. Samuel L. Dixon, *Working with People in Crisis*. St. Louis: C. V. Mosby, 1979, pp. 129–135.

10. Arnold, *op. cit.*, p. 269.

11. Michael E. Cavanagh, *The Experience of Counseling*. Monterey: Brooks/Cole, 1982, pp. 170–175.

12. Michael E. Cavanaugh, *What To Do When You Are Feeling Guilty*. Chicago: Claretian, 1978.

13. Dixon, *op. cit.*, pp. 152–156.

14. Dorothy Rethingshafer, *Motivation as Related to Personality*. New York: McGraw-Hill, 1963, pp. 150–155.

15. Andre Godin, S.J., *The Pastor as Counselor*. New York: Holt, Rinehart & Winston, 1965.

5. Coping Strategies

1. Richard S. Lazarus, "Coping Psychology," in *International Encyclopedia of Psychiatry, Psychology, Psychoanalysis, and Neurology*, Vol. 3. New York: Aesculapius, 1977, p. 379.

2. *Ibid.*

3. Gerald Caplan, *Principles of Preventive Psychiatry*. New York: Basic Books, 1964.

4. Karl A. Slaikeu, *Crisis Intervention*. Boston: Allyn and Bacon, Inc., 1984, p. 18.

5. James C. Coleman and C. L. Hammon, *Personality Dynamics and Effective Behavior*. Chicago: Foresman, Scott & Company, 1973.

6. Sigmund Freud, *The Problem of Anxiety*. New York: W. W. Norton & Company, 1936.

7. John Dollard and Neal E. Miller, *Personality and Psychotherapy*. New York: McGraw-Hill Company, 1950.

8. Coleman, *op. cit.*

9. Alexander A. Schneiders, *Personality Dynamics and Mental Health*. New York: Holt, Rinehart & Winston, 1965, p. 250.

10. Michael E. Cavanagh, *The Experience of Counseling*. Monterey: Brooks/Cole Publishing Company, 1982, p. 225.

11. Sigmund Freud, *A General Introduction to Psychoanalysis*. New York: Washington Square Press, 1960.

12. Cavanagh, *op. cit.*, pp. 225–226.

13. Coleman, *op. cit.*, pp. 203–204.

14. James M. Sawrey and Charles W. Telford, *Adjustment and Personality*. Boston: Allyn and Bacon, 1975, pp. 351–352.

15. Hiltner Seward, "Clinical and Theological Notes on Responsibility," *Journal of Religion and Health*, Vol. 2, 1962, pp. 7–20.

16. Carl R. Rogers, *On Becoming a Person*. Boston: Houghton-Mifflin, 1961, p. 54.

6. Listening and Responding to the Message

1. Lawrence M. Brammer, *The Helping Relationship* (3rd ed.). Englewood Cliffs: Prentice-Hall, 1985, pp. 65–66.

2. *Ibid.*, pp. 81–83.

3. *Ibid.*, pp. 74–75.

4. Michael E. Cavanagh, *The Counseling Experience*. Monterey: Brooks/Cole, 1982, pp. 157–159.

5. Gerard Egan, *The Skilled Helper* (2nd ed.). Monterey: Brooks/Cole, 1982, pp. 86–90.

6. Carl R. Rogers, *A Way of Being*. Boston: Houghton Mifflin, 1980, p. 142.

7. Egan, *op. cit.*, p. 88.

8. Rogers, *op. cit.*, pp. 144–145.

9. William H. Cormier and L. Sherilyn Cormier, *Interviewing Strategies for Helpers*. Monterey: Brooks/Cole, 1979, pp. 61–62.

10. Egan, *op. cit.*, pp. 58–72.

11. *Ibid.*, pp. 63–65.

12. Cavanagh, *op. cit.*, pp. 196–197.

13. David G. Martin, *Counseling and Therapy Skills*. Monterey: Brooks/Cole, 1983, pp. 3–16.

14. Alfred Benjamin, *The Helping Interview* (2nd ed.). Atlanta: Houghton Mifflin, 1974, pp. 67–69.

15. Brammer, *op. cit.*, pp. 69–70.

7. Influencing the Counselee

1. Allen E. Ivey, *Intentional Interviewing and Counseling*. Monterey: Brooks/Cole, 1983, p. 171.

2. William H. Cormier and L. Sherilyn Cormier, *Interviewing Strategies for Helpers*. Monterey: Brooks/Cole, 1979, p. 105.

3. *Ibid.*, p. 107.

4. *Ibid.*, p. 101.

5. *Ibid.*, p. 102.

6. Alfred Benjamin, *The Helping Interview* (2nd ed.). Boston: Houghton Mifflin, 1974, pp. 126–127.

7. Gerald Egan, *The Skilled Helper* (2nd ed.). Monterey: Brooks/Cole, 1982, p. 186.

8. *Ibid.*

9. Cormier and Cormier, *op. cit.*, pp. 84–86.

10. Lawrence M. Brammer, *The Helping Relationship* (3rd ed.). Englewood Cliffs: 1985, pp. 67–69.

11. *Ibid.*, p. 68.

12. *Ibid.*

13. Benjamin, *op. cit.*, p. 129.

14. *Ibid.*, p. 128.

15. Brammer, *op. cit.*, p. 88.

8. Problem Solving

1. Gerald Egan, *The Skilled Helper* (2nd ed.). Monterey: Brooks/Cole, 1982, pp. 86–87.

2. Lawrence M. Brammer, *The Helping Relationship* (3rd ed.). Englewood Cliffs: Prentice-Hall, 1979, pp. 69–70.

3. Alfred Benjamin, *The Helping Interview* (2nd ed.). Boston: Houghton Mifflin, 1974, pp. 67–69.

4. Allen E. Ivey, *Counseling and Psychotherapy*. Englewood Cliffs: Prentice-Hall, 1980, pp. 30–33.

5. Michael E. Cavanagh, *The Counseling Experience*. Monterey: Brooks/Cole, 1982, pp. 118–119.

6. Allen E. Ivey and Jerry Authier, *Microcounseling*. Springfield, Ill.: Charles C. Thomas, 1971, p. 209.

7. W. H. Cormier and L. S. Cormier, *Interviewing Strategies for Helpers*. Monterey: Brooks/Cole, 1979, pp. 165–168.

8. Egan, *op. cit.*, pp. 216–217.

9. *Ibid.*

10. *Ibid.*, pp. 214–216.

11. *Ibid.*, pp. 101–102.

12. David N. Dixon and John A. Glover, *Counseling: A Problem Solving Approach*. New York: John Wiley & Sons, 1984, pp. 93–99.

13. Robert R. Carkhuff, *The Art of Problem Solving*. Amherst, Mass.: Human Resources Development, 1974, pp. 91–116.

9. Supportive Measures

1. Alan J. Enelow, *Elements of Psychotherapy*. New York: Oxford University Press, 1977, p. 66.

2. Jack E. Hokanson, *Introduction to the Psychotherapeutic Process*. Reading, Mass.: Addison Wesley, 1983, p. 99.

3. Enelow, *ibid.*, p. 66.

4. H. I. Kaplan, A. M. Freedman, and B. J. Sadock, *Comprehensive Textbook of Psychiatry/III*, Vol. 2 Baltimore: 1980, p. 2138.

5. Polly Doyle, *Grief Counseling and Sudden Death*. Springfield, Ill.: Charles C. Thomas, 1980, p. 13.

6. *Ibid.*, p. 13.

7. Eric Lindemann, "Symptomotology and Management of Acute Grief," *American Journal of Psychiatry*, Vol. 101, September 1945, pp. 141–148.

8. Doyle, *ibid.*, pp. 162–164.

9. George Levinger and C. Moles, *Divorce and Separation*. New York: Basic Books, 1979, pp. 201–202.

10. *Ibid.*, 204.

11. John G. Cull and Richard E. Hardy, *Deciding on Divorce*. Springfield, Ill.: Charles C. Thomas, 1974, p. 35.

12. Levinger & Moles, *op. cit.*, p. 207.

13. Cull & Hardy, *op. cit.*, p. 34.

14. Mel Krantzler, *Creative Divorce*. New York: M. Evans, 1974, p. 16.

10. Stress and Crisis

1. Karl A. Slaikeu, *Crisis Intervention*. Boston: Allyn and Bacon, 1984, p. 13.

2. Samuel L. Dixon, *Working with People in Crisis*. St. Louis: C. V. Mosby, 1979, p. 10.

3. Slaikeu, *op. cit.*, pp. 14–15.

4. Dixon, *op. cit.*, p. 15.

5. Douglas A. Puryear, *Helping People in Crisis*. San Francisco: Jossey-Bass, 1979, p. 5.

6. Glenn E. Whitlock, *Understanding and Coping with Real-Life Crisis*. Monterey: Brooks/Cole, 1978, p. 121.

7. Michael E. Cavanagh, *The Counseling Experience*. Monterey: Brooks/Cole, 1982, pp. 321–323.

8. Dixon, *op. cit.*, pp. 87–88.

9. *Ibid.*, p. 120.

10. Lawrence M. Brammer, *The Helping Relationship* (2nd ed.). Englewood Cliffs: Prentice-Hall, 1979, pp. 81–83.

11. Making Referrals

1. Theodore Millon, *Disorders of Personality, DSM III: Axis II.* New York: John Wiley & Sons, 1981, p. 9.

2. *Diagnostic and Statistical Manual of Mental Disorders* (3rd ed.)— *DSM III*. Washington, D.C., 1980, pp. 196–198.

3. *Ibid.*, pp. 225–252.

4. *Ibid.*, pp. 210–218.

5. *Ibid.*, pp. 170–176.

6. *Ibid.*, pp. 317–320.

7. *Ibid.*, p. 320.

8. Karl A. Slaikeu, *Crisis Intervention*. Boston: Allyn and Bacon, 1984, p. 95.

9. Jill Miller, "Helping the Suicidal Client: Some Aspects of Assessment and Treatment," *Psychotherapy: Theory, Research and Practice*, 1980, 17, 94–100.

10. Samuel L. Dixon, *Working with People in Crisis*. St. Louis: C. V. Mosby, 1979, pp. 140–142.

11. James C. Coleman, James N. Butcher, and Robert C. Carlson, *Abnormal Psychology* (7th ed.). Glenview, Ill.: Scott, Foresman, 1980, pp. 129–140.

12. M. S. Peck, *The Road Less Traveled*. New York: Simon and Schuster, 1978, pp. 197–208.

13. Michael E. Cavanagh, *The Counseling Experience*. Monterey: Brooks/Cole, 1982, p. 3.

14. Clarence J. Bowe, *An Outline of Psychiatry*. Dubuque: Wm. C. Brown, 1984, pp. 35–47.

Suggested Readings

Adams, J.E. *Pastoral Counseling*. Grand Rapids: Baker Book House, 1975.

———. *Helps for Counselors*. Grand Rapids: Baker Book House, 1980.

Aguilera, D.C. and Messick, J.M. *Crisis Intervention* (2nd ed.). St. Louis: C.V. Mosby, 1974.

Albin, R.S. *Emotions*. Philadelphia: Westminster Press, 1983.

Arnold, W.V. *Introduction to Pastoral Care*. Philadelphia: Westminster, 1982.

Augsburger, D.W. *Anger and Assertiveness in Pastoral Care*. Philadelphia: Fortress, 1979.

Bailey, R.W. *Ministering to the Grieving*. Grand Rapids: Zondervan, 1980.

Barr, W.D. *Counseling with Confidence*. South Plainfield: Bridge, 1981.

Benjamin, A. *The Helping Interview* (2nd ed.). Atlanta: Houghton-Mifflin, 1974.

Berenson, B. and Mitchell, K. *Confrontation*. Amherst: Human Resources Development, 1974.

Bergendorff, C.L. *Pastoral Care for Alcoholism*. Center City, Minn.: Hazelden, 1981.

Bowe, C.J. *An Outline of Psychiatry*. Dubuque: William C. Brown, 1984.

Brammer, L.M. *The Helping Relationship* (3rd ed.). Englewood Cliffs: Prentice-Hall, 1979.

Carkhuff, R.R. *The Art of Helping III*. Amherst: Human Resources Development, 1973.

———. *The Art of Problem Solving*. Amherst: Human Resources Development, 1975.

———. *Teaching as Treatment*. Amherst: Human Resources Development, 1976.

Cavanagh, M.E. *What To Do When You Are Feeling Guilty*. Chicago: Claretian, 1978.

———. *The Counseling Experience*. Monterey: Brooks/Cole, 1982.

Clinebell, H. *Growth Counseling*. Nashville: Abingdon, 1979.

———. *Basic Types of Pastoral Care and Counseling*. Nashville: Abingdon, 1984.

Coleman, J.C. and Glaros, C. *Contemporary Psychology and Effective Behavior* (5th ed.). Glenview, Ill.: Scott, Foresman & Company, 1983.

———. *Abnormal Psychology* (7th ed.). Glenview, Ill.: Scott, Foresman, 1980.

Connolly, W.J. *Contemporary Spiritual Direction: Scope and Principles*. St. Louis: American Assistancy Seminar in Jesuit Spirituality, 1975.

Corey, G., Corey, M.S., and Callanan, P. *Issues and Ethics in the Helping Profession*. Monterey: Brooks/Cole, 1984.

Cormier, W.H. and Cormier, L.S. *Interviewing Strategies for Helpers*. Monterey: Brooks/Cole, 1979.

Curran, C.H. *Religious Values in Counseling and Psychotherapy*. New York: Sheed & Ward, 1969.

Danish, S. and Hauser, A. *Helping Skills: A Basic Training Program*. New York: Behavioral Publications, 1973.

Diagnostic & Statistical Manual of Mental Disorders—DSM III. Washington, D.C. American Psychiatric Association, 1980.

DiMattia, D. *Personal Communication*. Amherst: University of Massachusetts, 1970.

Dixon, D.M. and Glover, J.A. *Counseling: A Problem-Solving Approach*. New York: John Wiley, 1984.

Dixon, S. *Working with People in Crisis.* St. Louis: C.V. Mosby, 1979.

Duffy, R.A. *A Roman Catholic Theology of Pastoral Care.* Philadelphia: Fortess, 1983.

Egan, G. *The Skilled Helper* (2nd ed.). Monterey: Brooks/Cole, 1982.

Ekman, P. and Friesen W. *Unmasking the Face.* Englewood Cliffs: Prentice-Hall, 1975.

Enelow, A.J. *Elements of Psychotherapy.* New York: Oxford Press, 1977.

Faber, H. and Schoot, E. van der. *The Art of Pastoral Conversation.* Nashville: Abingdon, 1980.

Fairchild, R.W. *Finding Hope Again: A Pastor's Guide to Counseling Depressed People.* San Francisco: Harper & Row, 1980.

Farnsworth, D.L. and Braceland, F.J. *Psychiatry, the Clergy and Pastoral Counseling.* Collegeville, Minn.: St. John University Press, 1969.

Frankl, V. *Man's Search for Meaning.* New York: Simon & Schuster, 1959.

Gendlin, E.T. *Experiencing and Creation of Meaning.* New York: Free Press, 1962.

Gerkin, C.V. *Crisis Experience in Modern Life.* Nashville: Abingdon, 1979.

Godin, A. *The Pastor as Counselor.* New York: Holt, Rinehart & Winston, 1965.

Gordon, T. *Parent Effectiveness Training.* New York: Wyden, 1970.

Hall, E. *The Silent Language.* New York: Doubleday, 1959.

Hart, G.M. *Values Clarification for Counselors.* Springfield, Ill.: Charles C. Thomas, 1978.

Hart, T.N. *The Art of Christian Living.* New York: Paulist, 1980.

Hass, H.T. *Pastoral Counseling with People in Distress.* St. Louis: Concordia, 1969.

Hiltner, S. Pastoral Counseling (rev. ed.). Nashville: Abingdon, 1969.

———. *The Christian Shepherd: Some Aspects of Pastoral Care.* Nashville: Abingdon, 1980.

Hoffman, J.C. *Ethical Confrontation in Counseling.* Chicago: University of Chicago Press, 1979.

Hokanson, J.H. *Introduction to the Therapeutic Process.* Reading, Mass.: Addison-Wesley, 1983.

Hostie, R. *Pastoral Counseling*. New York: Sheed & Ward, 1960.

Hume, W.E. *How To Start Counseling*. Nashville: Abingdon, 1979.

———. *Pastoral Care and Counseling*. Columbus: Augsburg, 1981.

Ivey, A.E. *Intentional Interviewing and Counseling*. Monterey: Brooks/Cole, 1983.

Ivey, A.E. and Authier, J. *Microcounseling* (2nd ed.). Springfield, Ill.: Charles C. Thomas, 1969.

Ivey, A.E. and Litterer, J. *Face to Face*. Amherst: Consulting Group, 1979.

Ivey, A.E. and Simek-Downing, L. *Counseling and Psychotherapy*. Englewood Cliffs, NJ: Prentice-Hall, 1980.

Joy, E. *What Is Faith?* New York: Paulist, 1963.

Jourard, S. *Self-Disclosure*. New York: Wiley, 1971.

Kagan N. *Influencing Human Interaction*. East Lansing: Michigan State University, 1972.

Kelsey, M.T. *Prophetic Ministry*. New York: Crossroad, 1982.

Kennedy, E.C. *On Becoming a Counselor*. New York: Winston, 1977.

Keyes, P.T. *Pastoral Presence and the Diocesan Priest*. Whitinville, N.Y.: House of Affirmation, 1978.

Lee, R.R. *Clergy and Clients: The Practice of Pastoral Psychotherapy*. Oak Grove, Minn.: Winston, 1983.

Manson, R.L. *et al. The Clergyman and the Psychiatrist—When To Refer*. Chicago: Nelson-Hall, 1978.

Martin, D.G. *Counseling and Therapy Skills*. Monterey: Brooks/Cole, 1983.

Maslow, A. *The Further Reaches of Human Nature*. New York: Viking, 1971.

McKay, M., Davis, M. and Fanning, P. *Messages: The Communication Book*. Oakland: New Harbinger, 1983.

Mehrabian, A. *Nonverbal Communication*. New York: Adline-Atherton, 1972.

Millon, T. *Disorders of Personality, DSM III: Axis II*. New York: Wiley, 1981.

Niklas, G.R. *Ministry to the Sick* (2nd ed.). Staten Island, N.Y.: Alba House, 1982.

Oglesby, W.B. *Referral in Pastoral Counseling*. Nashville: Abingdon, 1978.

Oates, W.E. *Pastor's Handbook*, Vol. I & II. Philadelphia: Westminister, 1980.

———. *The Christian Pastor* (3rd ed.). Philadelphia: Westminister, 1982.

Peterson, E. *Who Cares? A Handbook of Christian Counseling*. Wilton, Conn.: Morehouse, 1982.

Puryear, D.A. *Helping People in Crisis*. San Francisco: Jossey-Bass, 1979.

Reynolds, D.K. and Farberow, N.L. *Suicide Inside and Out*. Berkeley: University of California Press, 1970.

Rightor, H.H. *Counseling in Work Crisis*. Valley Forge: Judson, 1979.

Rogers, C.R. *Client-Centered Therapy*. Boston: Houghton-Mifflin, 1951.

———. *On Becoming a Person*. Boston: Houghton-Mifflin, 1961.

———. *A Way of Being*. Boston: Houghton-Mifflin, 1980.

Schoenberg, B., Gerber, I., Kutscher, A.H., Peretz, D., and Carr, A.C. *Bereavement: Its Psychosocial Aspects*. New York: Columbia University Press, 1975.

Seymour, S. and Bradburn, N.M. *Asking Questions*. San Francisco: Jossey-Bass, 1982.

Slaikeu, K.A. *Crisis Intervention: A Handbook of Practice and Research*. Boston: Allyn & Bacon, 1984.

Smith, M. *Value Clarification*. La Jolla: University Associates, 1977.

Soulen, R.N. *Care for the Dying*. Atlanta: John Knox, 1975.

Sue, D. *Counseling the Culturally Different*. New York: Wiley, 1981.

Tyler, L. *The Work of a Counselor*. New York: Appleton, 1953.

Vanderpool, J.A. *People in Pain: A Guide to Pastoral Care*. Springfield, Ill.: Charles C. Thomas, 1979.

Weiner, M. and Mehrabian, A. *Language Within Language: Immediacy, a Channel in Verbal Communication*. New York: Appleton, 1968.

Whitlock, G.E. *Understanding and Coping with Real-Life Problems*. Monterey: Brooks/Cole, 1978.

Wimberly, E.P. *Pastoral Counseling and Spiritual Values*. Nashville: Abingdon, 1982.

Wynn, J.C. *Family Therapy in Pastoral Ministry*. San Francisco: Harper & Row, 1982.